Dragon in the Tunnel

Ruskin Bond has been writing for over sixty years, and now has over 120 titles in print—novels, collections of short stories, poetry, essays, anthologies and books for children. His first novel, *The Room on the Roof*, received the prestigious John Llewellyn Rhys Prize in 1957. He has also received the Padma Shri (1999), the Padma Bhushan (2014) and two awards from Sahitya Akademi—one for his short stories and another for his writings for children. In 2012, the Delhi government gave him its Lifetime Achievement Award.

Born in 1934, Ruskin Bond grew up in Jamnagar, Shimla, New Delhi and Dehradun. Apart from three years in the UK, he has spent all his life in India, and now lives in Mussoorie with his adopted family.

RUSKIN BOND

Dragon in the Tunnel

RUPA

Published by
Rupa Publications India Pvt. Ltd 2017
7/16, Ansari Road, Daryaganj
New Delhi 110002

Sales centres:
Allahabad Bengaluru Chennai
Hyderabad Jaipur Kathmandu
Kolkata Mumbai

ISBN: 978-81-291-4918-3

First impression 2017

10 9 8 7 6 5 4 3 2 1

Printed and bound in India by Repro Knowledgecast Limited, Thane

Contents

Introduction

Memories become the fondest part of our lives as we grow old. Take it from someone who is not so young anymore. And I spend a good part of my days in nostalgia. I can be found reminiscing mostly about smaller towns, fewer people, lesser technologies, and simpler lives; of days full of pleasure and peace.

Here I have put together some of my recollections of a time gone by. It is 2017 now, but these stories will take you on a trip to the 1950s and 60s. The sparsely populated Delhi and Dehra of those days make for some of the best memories of my childhood and youth. I first lived in Delhi in the early 40s with my father, and I shall never forget the fragrant, refreshing smell of the wet khas-reed which cooled the rooms and verandahs of New Delhi bungalows. What helped me survive that summer was the box-like wind-up gramophone on which I played endless records which had to be stored flat in order to prevent them from warping and assuming weird shapes in the heat.

In the late 50s I returned to live again in Delhi, this time as a freelance writer. That is when I came to like things about the city even during its summer. The smell of a hot Indian summer is one smell that can never be forgotten. For who can forget that summer brings the jasmine, whose sweet scent drifts past us on the evening breeze along with the stronger odours and scents of mango blossom, raat-ki-rani and cow dung smoke. And while I was in Delhi I would sometimes travel to nearby towns. Once I went to Meerut just when the monsoon was about to break and when it did—the landscape dappled with light and shade, dark islands of cloud moved across the bright green fields, the effect of which on one's spirits was strangely exhilarating.

In Delhi, I mostly stayed with a friend's family. They were a large Punjabi family living in Rajouri Garden of west Delhi. Warm-hearted as they were, their idiosyncrasies never failed to entertain me. It is their eccentricities which fill up most of the entries in my journal from that period. Eventually, I returned to Dehra. Though I had become quite fond of Delhi, my roots were always calling me back. In Dehra, I spent most of my time walking about the town looking for my childhood memories in its faintest corners. I grew up in Dehra. My grandfather had built a bungalow on the outskirts of the town at the turn of the century. The house was sold a few years after Independence. No one remembered that when I returned, for it was over twenty years since I had left the place, and my boyhood friends were scattered and lost. And although the India of Kim was no more, and the Grand Trunk Road was now a procession of trucks instead of a slow-moving caravan of horses and camels, India was still a country in which people were easily lost and quickly forgotten.

But I do not forget old friends, old love, old places, and here are a few of them preserved in words and vivid memories.

Ruskin Bond

Summertime in Old New Delhi

I left Dehra for Delhi in 1959, and lived in the capital for a few years—freelancing, and for a time working with an international relief agency. I could not fall in love with Delhi, my heart was always in the hills and small towns of North India.

But there were things I came to like about Delhi, even in summer. The smell of a hot Indian summer is one smell that can never be forgotten. It is not just the thirsty earth with its distinctive odour, but all other ingredients of a hot weather in the plains that go to make this season almost intolerable on the one hand and sweetly memorable on the other. For who can forget that summer brings the jasmine, whose sweet scent drifts past us on the evening breeze along with the stronger odours and scents of mango blossom, raat-ki-rani and cowdung smoke.

Although I have spent most of my life in the hills, I grew up in some fairly hot places—humid Kathiawar ports, dusty old New Delhi, and the steamy Terai—and I am no stranger to prickly heat, mosquito bites, intermittent fever and dysentery and other hot weather afflictions. Today's residents of the capital complain of pollution and overcrowding, and I wouldn't exchange my mountain perch for the pleasure of being fried crisp, but at least half of them have air-conditioning, coolers, refrigerators and other means to keep the heat at bay. In 1940s' Delhi you were lucky to have a small table-fan, and that was effective only if the bhisti, or water-carrier, came around with his goat-skin bag, splashing water on to the khas-khas matting draped from your door or window; otherwise the fan simply blew hot air at you. I was in Delhi in the early '40s, living with my father, and I shall never forget the fragrant, refreshing smell of the wet khas-reed which cooled the rooms and verandahs of New Delhi bungalows (the only high-rise building was the Qutab Minar).

My father and I lived in a small RAF hutment on the fringe of the scrub jungle near Humayun's tomb. This was then furthest Delhi, where one could expect to find peacocks in the garden and a snake in the bathroom. The bhisti and the khas-khas helped us to survive that summer. As did the box-like wind-up gramophone on which I played endless records which had to be stored flat in order to prevent them from warping and assuming weird shapes in the heat. My father liked opera, and on his day off he would play his Caruso records. It was strange to lie beside him on a perspiration-soaked bed, listening to Caruso sing *Che Gelida Manina:*

Your tiny hand is frozen,
Let me warm it into life!

I was nine, a child of warm climates, and I had no idea what it was like to have one's hand frozen. Dipping my hands in ice cream was the nearest I'd come to it.

In 1959 I was living on the outskirts of a greater, further New Delhi. The influx of refugees from the Punjab after Partition had led to many new colonies springing up on the outskirts of the capital, and at the time the furthest of these was Rajouri Garden. Needless to say, there were no gardens. The treeless colony was buffeted by hot, dusty winds from Haryana and Rajasthan. The houses were built on one side of the Najafgarh Road. On the other side, as yet uncolonized, were extensive fields of wheat and other crops still belonging to the original inhabitants. In an attempt to escape the city life that constantly oppressed me, I would walk across the main road and into the fields, finding old wells, irrigation channels, camels and buffaloes, and sighting birds and small creatures that no longer dwelt in the city. In an odd way, it was my reaction to city life that led to my taking a greater interest in the natural world. Up to that time, I had taken it all for granted.

The notebook I kept at the time is before me now, and my first entry describes the bluejays or rollers that were so much a feature of those remaining open spaces. At rest, the bird is fairly nondescript, but when it takes flight it reveals the glorious bright blue wings and the tail, banded with a lighter blue. It sits motionless. But the large dark eyes are constantly watching the ground in every direction. A grasshopper or cricket has only to make a brief appearance, and the bluejay will launch itself straight at its prey. In the spring and early summer the 'roller' lives up to its other name. It indulges in love flights in which it rises and falls in the air with harsh grating screams—a real rock-'n'-roller!

Some way down the Najafgarh Road was a large village pond and beside it a magnificent banyan tree. We have no place for banyan trees today, they need so much space in which to spread their limbs and live comfortably. Cut away its aerial roots and the great tree topples over—usually to make way for a spacious apartment building. That was the first banyan tree I got to know really well. It had about a hundred pillars supporting the boughs, and above them there was this great leafy crown like a pillared hall. It has been said that whole armies could shelter in the shade of an old banyan. And probably at one time they did. I saw another sort of army visit the banyan by the village pond when it was in fruit. Parakeets, mynas, rosy pastors, crested bulbuls without crests, barbets and many other birds crowded the tree in order to feast noisily on big, scarlet figs. Season's eatings!

Even further down the Najafgarh Road was a large jheel, famous for its fishing. I wonder if any part of the jheel still exists, or if it got filled in and became a part of greater Delhi. One could rest in the shade of a small babul or keekar tree and watch the kingfisher skim over the water, making just a slight splash as it dived and came up with small glistening fishes. Our common Indian kingfisher is a beautiful little bird with a brilliant blue back, a white throat and orange underparts. I would spot one perched on an overhanging bush or rock, and wait to see it plunge like an arrow into the water and return to its perch to devour the catch. It came over the water in a flash of gleaming blue, shrilling its loud 'tit-tit-tit'.

The kingfisher is the subject of a number of legends, and the one I remember best, recounted by Romain Rolland, tells us that it was originally a plain grey bird that acquired its resplendent colours by flying straight towards the sun when Noah let it out of the Ark. Its upper plumage took the colour of the sky above, while the lower was scorched a deep russet by the rays of the setting sun.

Summer and winter, I scorned the dust and the traffic, and walked all over Delhi—from Rajouri Garden to Connaught Place, which must have been five or six miles, and on other occasions, from Daryaganj to Chandni Chowk, and from Ajmeri Gate to India Gate! That is the best way to get to know a city. I had walked all over London. Now I did the same thing in Delhi, investigating old tombs and monuments, historic streets and buildings, or simply sitting on the grass near India Gate and eating jamuns. I liked the sour tang of the jamun fruit which is best eaten with a little salt. And I liked the deep purple colour of the fruit. Jamuns were one of the nicer things about Delhi.

Break of the Monsoon

From Delhi I made occasional forays into nearby towns. Meerut was one of the towns I travelled to, and there, one evening, I saw the magic of the monsoon.

I was staying at a small hotel. There had been no rain for a month, but the atmosphere was humid, there were clouds overhead, dark clouds burgeoning with moisture. Thunder blossomed in the air.

The monsoon was going to break that day. I knew it; the birds knew it; the grass knew it. There was the smell of rain in the air. And the grass, the birds and I responded to this odour with the same sensuous longing.

A large drop of water hit the windowsill, darkening the thick dust on the woodwork. A faint breeze had sprung up, and again I felt the moisture, closer and warmer.

Then the rain approached like a dark curtain.

I could see it marching down the street, heavy and remorseless. It drummed on the corrugated tin roof and swept across the road and over the balcony of my room. I sat there without moving, letting the rain soak my sticky shirt and gritty hair.

Outside, the street rapidly emptied. The crowd dissolved in

the rain. Then buses, cars and bullock carts ploughed through the suddenly rushing water. A group of small boys, gloriously naked, came romping along a side street, which was like a river in spate. A garland of marigolds, swept off the steps of a temple, came floating down the middle of the road.

The rain stopped as suddenly as it had begun. The day was dying, and the breeze remained cool and moist. In the brief twilight that followed, I was witness to the great yearly flight of insects into the cool brief freedom of the night.

Termites and white ants, which had been sleeping through the hot season, emerged from their lairs. Out of every hole and crack, and from under the roots of trees, huge winged ants emerged, fluttering about heavily on this, the first and last flight of their lives. There was only one direction in which they could fly—towards the light, towards the street lights and the bright neon tube light above my balcony.

The light above the balcony attracted a massive, quivering swarm of clumsy termites, giving the impression of one thick, slowly revolving mass. A frog had found its way through the bathroom and came hopping across the balcony to pause beneath the light. All he had to do was gobble, as insects fell around him.

This was the hour of the geckos, the wall lizards. They had their reward for weeks of patient waiting. Plying their sticky pink tongues, they devoured insects as swiftly and methodically as children devour popcorn. For hours they crammed their stomachs, knowing that such a feast would not come their way again. Throughout the entire hot season the insect world had prepared for this flight out of darkness into light, and the phenomenon would not happen again for another year.

In hot upcountry towns in India it is good to have the

first monsoon showers arrive at night, while you are sleeping on the verandah. You wake up to the scent of wet earth and fallen neem leaves, and find that a hot and stuffy bungalow has been converted into a cool, damp place. The swish of the banana fronds and the drumming of the rain on broad-leaved sal trees will soothe the most fevered brow.

During the rains the frogs have a perfect Country Music Festival. There are two sets of them, it seems, and they sing antiphonal chants all evening, each group letting the other take its turn in the fairest manner. No one sees or hears them during the hot weather, but the moment the monsoon breaks they swarm all over the place.

When night comes on, great moths fly past, and beetles of all shapes and sizes come whirring in at the open windows. Recently, when Prem closed my window to keep out these winged visitors, I remonstrated, saying that as a nature lover I would share my room with them. I'd forgotten that I am inclined to sleep with my mouth open. In the wee hours I woke up, spluttering and choking, to find that I had almost swallowed a large and somewhat unpleasant tasting moth. I closed the window. Moths are lovely creatures, but a good night's sleep is even lovelier.

At night the fireflies light up their lamps, flashing messages to each other through the mango groves. Some nocturnal insects thrive mainly at the expense of humans. Sometimes, one wakes up to find thirty or forty mosquitoes looking through the netting in a bloodthirsty manner. If you are sleeping out, you will need that mosquito netting.

The road outside is lined with fine babul trees, now covered with powdery little balls of yellow blossom, filling the air with a faint scent. After the first showers there is a great deal of water about, and for many miles the trees are standing in it.

The common monsoon sights along an upcountry road are often picturesque—the wide plains, with great herds of smoke-coloured, delicate-limbed cattle being driven slowly home for the night, accompanied by troops of ungainly buffaloes and flocks of black long-tailed sheep. Then you come to a pond, where the buffaloes are indulging in a sensuous wallow, no part of them visible but the tips of their noses.

Within a few days of the first rain the air is full of dragonflies, crossing and recrossing, poised motionless for a moment, then darting away with that mingled grace and power which is unmatched among insects. Dragonflies are the swallows of the insect world; their prey is the mosquito, the gnat, the midge and the fly. These swarms, therefore, tell us that the moistened surface of the ground, with its mouldering leaves and sodden grass, has become one vast incubator teeming with every form of ephemeral life.

After the monotony of a fierce sun and a dusty landscape quivering in the dim distance, one welcomes these days of mild light, green earth and purple hills coming nearer in the clear and transparent air.

And later on, when the monsoon begins to break up and the hills are dappled with light and shade, dark islands of cloud moving across the bright green sea, the effect on one's spirits is strangely exhilarating.

Bhabiji's House

(My neighbours in Rajouri Garden back in the 1960s were the Kamal family. This entry from my journal, which 1 wrote on one of my later visits, describes a typical day in that household.)

At first light there is a tremendous burst of birdsong from the guava tree in the little garden. Over a hundred sparrows wake up all at once and give tongue to whatever it is that sparrows have to say to each other at five o'clock on a foggy winter's morning in Delhi.

In the small house, people sleep on; that is, everyone except 'Bhabiji'—Granny—the head of the lively Punjabi middle-class family with whom I nearly always stay when I am in Delhi.

She coughs, stirs, groans, grumbles and gets out of bed. The fire has to be lit, and food prepared for two of her sons to take to work. There is her daughter-in-law, Shobha, to help her; but the girl is not very bright at getting up in the morning. Actually, it is this way: Bhabiji wants to show up her daughter-in-law; so, no matter how hard Shobha tries to be up first, Bhabiji forestalls her. The old lady does not sleep well, anyway; her eyes are open long before the first sparrow chirps, and as soon as she sees her daughter-in-law stirring, she scrambles out of bed and hurries to the kitchen. This gives her the opportunity to say: 'What good is a daughter-in-law when I have to get up to prepare her husband's food?'

The truth is that Bhabiji does not like anyone else preparing her sons' food. She looks no older than when I first saw her ten years ago. She still has complete control over a large family and, with tremendous confidence and enthusiasm, presides over the lives of three sons, a daughter, two daughters-in-law and fourteen grandchildren. This is a joint family (there are not many left in a big city like Delhi), in which the sons and their families all live together as one unit under their mother's benevolent (and sometimes slightly malevolent) autocracy. Even when her husband was alive, Bhabiji dominated the household.

The eldest son, Shiv, has a separate kitchen, but his wife and children participate in all the family celebrations and quarrels. It is a small miracle how everyone (including myself when I visit) manages to fit into the house; and a stranger might be forgiven for wondering where everyone sleeps, for no beds are visible during the day. That is because the beds—light wooden frames with rough string across—are brought in only at night, and are taken out first thing in the morning and kept in the garden shed.

As Bhabiji lights the kitchen fire, the household begins to stir, and Shobha joins her mother-in-law in the kitchen. As a guest I am privileged and may get up last. But my bed soon becomes an island battered by waves of scurrying, shouting children, eager to bathe, dress, eat and find their school books. Before I can get up, someone brings me a tumbler of hot sweet tea. It is a brass tumbler and burns my fingers; I have yet to learn how to hold one properly. Punjabis like their tea with lots of milk and sugar—so much so that I often wonder why they bother to add any tea.

Ten years ago, 'bed tea' was unheard of in Bhabiji's house. Then, the first time I came to stay, Kamal, the youngest son, told Bhabiji: 'My friend is Angrez. He must have tea in bed.' He forgot to mention that I usually took my morning cup at seven; they gave it to me at five. I gulped it down and went to sleep again. Then, slowly, others in the household began indulging in morning cups of tea. Now everyone, including the older children, has 'bed tea'. They bless my English forebears for instituting the custom; I bless the Punjabis for perpetuating it.

Breakfast is by rota, in the kitchen. It is a tiny room and accommodates only four adults at a time. The children have eaten first; but the smallest children, Shobha's toddlers, keep coming in and climbing over us. Says Bhabiji of the youngest and most mischievous: 'He lives only because God keeps a special eye on him.'

Kamal, his elder brother Arun and I sit cross-legged and barefooted on the floor while Bhabiji serves us hot parathas stuffed with potatoes and onions, along with omelettes, an excellent dish. Arun then goes to work on his scooter, while Kamal catches a bus for the city, where he attends an art college. After they have gone, Bhabiji and Shobha have their breakfast.

By nine o'clock everyone who is still in the house is busy doing something. Shobha is washing clothes. Bhabiji has settled down on a cot with a huge pile of spinach, which she methodically cleans and chops up. Madhu, her fourteen-year-old granddaughter, who attends school only in the afternoons, is washing down the sitting room floor. Madhu's mother is a teacher in a primary school in Delhi, and earns a pittance of Rs 150 a month. Her husband went to England ten years ago, and never returned; he does not send any money home.

Madhu is made attractive by the gravity of her countenance. She is always thoughtful, reflective; seldom speaks, smiles rarely (but looks very pretty when she does). I wonder what she thinks about as she scrubs floors, prepares meals with Bhabiji, washes dishes and even finds a few hard-pressed moments for her schoolwork. She is the Cinderella of the house. Not that she has to put up with anything like a cruel stepmother. Madhu is Bhabiji's favourite. She has made herself so useful that she is above all reproach. Apart from that, there is a certain measure of aloofness about her—she does not get involved in domestic squabbles—and this is foreign to a household in which everyone has something to say for himself or herself. Her two young brothers are constantly being reprimanded; but no one says anything to Madhu. Only yesterday morning, when clothes were being washed and Madhu was scrubbing the floor, the following dialogue took place.

Madhu's mother (picking up a school book left in the courtyard): 'Where's that boy Popat? See how careless he is with his books! Popat! He's run off. Just wait till he gets back. I'll give him a good beating.'

Vinod's mother: 'It's not Popat's book. It's Vinod's. Where's Vinod?'

Vinod (grumpily): 'It's Madhu's book.'

Silence for a minute or two. Madhu continues scrubbing the floor; she does not bother to look up. Vinod picks up the book and takes it indoors. The women return to their chores.

Manju, daughter of Shiv and sister of Vinod, is averse to housework and, as a result, is always being scolded—by her parents, grandmother, uncles and aunts.

Now, she is engaged in the unwelcomed chore of sweeping the front yard. She does this with a sulky look, ignoring my cheerful remarks. I have been sitting under the guava tree, but Manju soon sweeps me away from this spot. She creates a drifting cloud of dust, and seems satisfied only when the dust settles on the clothes that have just been hung up to dry. Manju is a sensuous creature and, like most sensuous people, is lazy by nature. She does not like sweeping because the boy next door can see her at it, and she wants to appear before him in a more glamorous light. Her first action every morning is to turn to the cinema advertisements in the newspaper. Bombay's movie moguls cater for girls like Manju who long to be tragic heroines. Life is so very dull for middle-class teenagers in Delhi that it is only natural that they should lean so heavily on escapist entertainment. Every residential area has a cinema. But there is not a single bookshop in this particular suburb, although it has a population of over twenty thousand literate people. Few children read books; but they are adept at swotting up examination 'guides'; and students of, say, Hardy or Dickens read the guides and not the novels.

Bhabiji is now grinding onions and chillies in a mortar. Her eyes are watering but she is in a good mood. Shobha sits quietly in the kitchen. A little while ago she was complaining to me of a backache. I am the only one who lends a sympathetic ear to complaints of aches and pains. But since last night, my sympathies have been under severe strain. When I got into bed at about ten o'clock, I found the sheets wet. Apparently Shobha had put her baby to sleep in my bed during the afternoon.

While the housework is still in progress, cousin Kishore arrives. He is an itinerant musician who makes a living by arranging performances at weddings. He visits Bhabiji's house frequently and at odd hours, often a little tipsy, always brimming over with goodwill and grandiose plans for the future. It was once his ambition to be a film producer, and some years back he lost a lot of Bhabiji's money in producing a film that was never completed. He still talks of finishing it.

'Brother,' he says, taking me into his confidence for the hundredth time, 'do you know anyone who has a movie camera?'

'No,' I say, knowing only too well how these admissions can lead me into a morass of complicated manoeuvres. But Kishore is not easily put off, especially when he has been fortified with country liquor.

'But you *knew* someone with a movie camera?' He asks.

'That was long ago.'

'How long ago?' (I have got him going now.)

'About five years back.'

'Only five years? Find him, find him!'

'It's no use. He doesn't have the movie camera any more. He sold it.'

'Sold it!' Kishore looks at me as though I have done him an injury. 'But why didn't you buy it? All we need is a movie camera, and our fortune is made. I will produce the film, I will direct it, I will write the music. Two in one, Charlie Chaplin and Raj Kapoor. Why didn't you buy the camera?'

'Because I didn't have the money.'

'But we could have borrowed the money.'

'If you are in a position to borrow money, you can go out and buy another movie camera.'

'We could have borrowed the camera. Do you know anyone else who has one?'

'Not a soul.' I am firm this time; I will not be led into another maze.

'Very sad, very sad,' mutters Kishore. And with a dejected, hangdog expression designed to make me feel that I am responsible for all his failures, he moves off.

Bhabiji had expressed some annoyance at his arrival, but

he softens her up by leaving behind an invitation to a wedding party this evening. No one in the house knows the bride's or bridegroom's family, but that does not matter; knowing one of the musicians is just as good. Almost everyone will go.

While Bhabiji, Shobha and Madhu are preparing lunch, Bhabiji engages in one of her favourite subjects of conversation, Kamal's marriage, which she hopes she will be able to arrange in the near future. She freely acknowledges that she made grave blunders in selecting wives for her other sons—this is meant to be heard by Shobha—and promises not to repeat her mistakes. According to Bhabiji, Kamal's bride should be both educated and domesticated; and of course she must be fair.

'What if he likes a dark girl?' I ask teasingly.

Bhabiji looks horrified. 'He cannot marry a dark girl,' she declares.

'But dark girls are beautiful,' I tell her.

'Impossible!'

'Do you want him to marry a European girl?'

'No foreigners! I know them, they'll take my son away. He shall have a good Punjabi girl, with a complexion the colour of wheat.'

Noon. The shadows shift and cross the road. I sit beneath the guava tree and watch the women at work. They will not let me do anything, but they like talking to me and they love to hear my broken Punjabi. Sparrows flit about at their feet, snapping up the grain that runs away from their busy fingers. A crow looks speculatively at the empty kitchen, sidles towards the open door; but Bhabiji has only to glance up and the experienced crow flies away. He knows he will not be able to make off with anything from this house.

One by one the children come home, demanding food. Now it is Madhu's turn to go to school. Her younger brother

Popat, an intelligent but undersized boy of thirteen, appears in the doorway and asks for lunch.

'Be off!' says Bhabiji. 'It isn't ready yet.'

Actually the food is ready and only the chapatis remain to be made. Shobha will attend to them. Bhabiji lies down on her cot in the sun, complaining of a pain in her back and ringing noises in her ears.

'I'll press your back,' says Popat. He has been out of Bhabiji's favour lately, and is looking for an opportunity to be rehabilitated.

Barefooted he stands on Bhabiji's back and treads her weary flesh and bones with a gentle walking-in-one-spot movement. Bhabiji grunts with relief. Every day she has new pains in new places. Her age, and the daily business of feeding the family and running everyone's affairs, are beginning to tell on her. But she would sooner die than give up her position of dominance in the house. Her working sons still hand over their pay to her, and she dispenses the money as she sees fit.

The pummelling she gets from Popat puts her in a better mood, and she holds forth on another favourite subject, the respective merits of various dowries. Shiv's wife (according to Bhabiji) brought nothing with her but a string cot; Kishore's wife brought only a sharp and clever tongue; Shobha brought a wonderful steel cupboard, fully expecting that it would do all the housework for her.

This last observation upsets Shobha, and a little later I find her under the guava tree, weeping profusely. I give her the comforting words she obviously expects; but it is her husband Arun who will have to bear the brunt of her outraged feelings when he comes home this evening. He is rather nervous of his wife. Last night he wanted to eat out, at a restaurant, but did not want to be accused of wasting money; so he stuffed fifteen rupees into my pocket and asked me to invite both him and Shobha to dinner, which I did.

We had a good dinner. Such unexpected hospitality on my part has further improved my standing with Shobha. Now, in spite of other chores, she sees that I get cups of tea and coffee at odd hours of the day.

Bhabiji knows Arun is soft with his wife, and taunts him about it. She was saying this morning that whenever there is any work to be done Shobha retires to bed with a headache (partly true). She says even Manju does more housework (not true). Bhabiji has certain talents as an actress, and does a good take-off of Shobha sulking and grumbling at having too much to do.

While Bhabiji talks, Popat sneaks off and goes for a ride on the bicycle. It is a very old bicycle and is constantly undergoing repairs. 'The soul has gone out of it,' says Vinod philosophically and makes his way on to the roof, where he keeps a store of pornographic literature. Up there, he cannot be seen and cannot be remembered, and so avoids being sent out on errands.

One of the boys is bathing at the handpump. Manju, who should have gone to school with Madhu, is stretched out on a cot, complaining of fever. But she will be up in time to attend the wedding party…

Towards evening, as the birds return to roost in the guava tree, their chatter is challenged by the tumult of people in the house getting ready for the wedding party.

Manju presses her tight pyjamas but neglects to darn them. She wears a loose-fitting, diaphanous shirt. She keeps flitting in and out of the front room so that I can admire the way she glitters. Shobha has used too much powder and lipstick in an effort to look like the femme fatale which she indubitably is not. Shiv's more conservative wife floats around in loose, old-fashioned pyjamas. Bhabiji is sober and austere in a white sari. Madhu looks neat. The men wear their suits.

Popat is holding up a mirror for his Uncle Kishore, who is combing his long hair. (Kishore kept his hair long, like a court musician at the time of Akbar, before the hippies had been heard of.) He is nodding benevolently, having fortified himself from a bottle labelled 'Som Ras' ('Nectar of the Gods'), obtained cheaply from an illicit still.

Kishore: 'Don't shake the mirror, boy!'

Popat: 'Uncle, it's your head that's shaking.'

Shobha is happy. She loves going out, especially to weddings, and she always takes her two small boys with her, although they invariably spoil the carpets.

Only Kamal, Popat and I remain behind. I have had more than my share of wedding parties.

The house is strangely quiet. It does not seem so small now, with only three people left in it. The kitchen has been locked (Bhabiji will not leave it open while Popat is still in the house), so we visit the dhaba, the wayside restaurant near the main road, and this time I pay the bill with my own money. We have kababs and chicken curry.

Yesterday Kamal and I took our lunch on the grass of the Buddha Jayanti Gardens (Buddha's Birthday Gardens). There was no college for Kamal, as the majority of Delhi's students had hijacked a number of corporation buses and headed for the Pakistan High Commission, with every intention of levelling it to the ground if possible, as a protest against the hijacking of an Indian plane from Srinagar to Lahore. The students were met by the Delhi police in full strength, and a pitched battle took place, in which stones from the students and tear gas shells from the police were the favoured missiles. There were two shells fired every minute, according to a newspaper report. And this went on all day. A number of students and policemen were injured, but by some miracle no one was killed. The police held their ground, and the Pakistan High Commission remained inviolate. But the Australian High Commission, situated to the rear of the student brigade, received most of the tear gas shells, and had to close down for the day.

Kamal and I attended the siege for about an hour, before retiring to the Gardens with our ham sandwiches. A couple of friendly squirrels came up to investigate, and were soon taking bread from our hands. We could hear the chanting of the students in the distance. I lay back on the grass and opened my copy of *Barchester Towers*. Whenever life in Delhi, or in Bhabiji's house (or anywhere, for that matter), becomes too tumultuous, I turn to Trollope. Nothing could be further removed from the turmoil of our times than an English cathedral town in the nineteenth century. But I think Jane Austen would have appreciated life in Bhabiji's house.

By ten o'clock, everyone is back from the wedding. (They had gone for the feast, and not for the ceremonies, which continue into the early hours of the morning.) Shobha is full of praise for the bridegroom's good looks and fair complexion. She describes him as being 'gora-chitta'—very white! She does not have a high opinion of the bride.

Shiv, in a happy and reflective mood, extols the qualities of his own wife, referring to her as the Barrel. He tells us how, shortly after their marriage, she had threatened to throw a brick at the next-door girl. This little incident remains fresh in Shiv's mind, after eighteen years of marriage.

He says: 'When the neighbours came and complained, I told them, "It is quite possible that my wife will throw a brick at your daughter. She is in the habit of throwing bricks." The neighbours held their peace.'

I think Shiv is rather proud of his wife's militancy when it comes to taking on neighbours; recently she vanquished the woman next door (a formidable Sikh lady) after a verbal battle that lasted three hours. But in arguments or quarrels with Bhabiji, Shiv's wife always loses, because Shiv takes his mother's side. Arun, on the other hand, is afraid of both wife and mother, and simply makes himself scarce when a quarrel develops. Or he tells his mother she is right, and then, to placate Shobha, takes her to the pictures.

Kishore turns up just as everyone is about to go to bed. Bhabiji is annoyed at first, because he has been drinking too much; but when he produces a bunch of cinema tickets, she is mollified and asks him to stay the night. Not even Bhabiji likes missing a new picture.

Kishore is urging me to write his life story.

'Your life would make a most interesting story,' I tell him. 'But it will be interesting only if I put in everything—your successes *and* your failures.'

'No, no, only successes,' exhorts Kishore. 'I want you to describe me as a popular music director.'

'But you have yet to become popular.'

'I will be popular if you write about me.'

Fortunately we are interrupted by the cots being brought in. Then Bhabiji and Shiv go into a huddle, discussing plans for building an extra room. After all, Kamal may be married soon.

One by one, the children get under their quilts. Popat starts massaging Bhabiji's back. She gives him her favourite blessing: 'God protect you and give you lots of children.' If God listens to all of Bhabiji's prayers and blessings, there will never be a fall in the population.

The lights are off and Bhabiji settles down for the night.

She is almost asleep when a small voice pipes up: 'Bhabiji, tell us a story.'

At first Bhabiji pretends not to hear; then, when the request is repeated, she says: 'You'll keep Aunty Shobha awake, and then she'll have an excuse for getting up late in the morning.' But the children know Bhabiji's one great weakness, and they renew their demand.

'Your grandmother is tired,' says Arun. 'Let her sleep.'

But Bhabiji's eyes are open. Her mind is going back over the crowded years, and she remembers something very interesting that happened when her younger brother's wife's sister married the eldest son of her third cousin…

Before long, the children are asleep, and I am wondering if I will ever sleep, for Bhabiji's voice drones on, into the darker reaches of the night.

Walking the Streets of Delhi

I made my home in Mussoorie in 1963, but of course I was to revisit Delhi many times, even spending a couple of winters there.

On one of these visits, in 1971, I reached my friend Kamal's house in Rajouri Garden, and mentioned that I had walked from Connaught Place, a distance of some eight miles. His family greeted me with a pained and bewildered silence.

Finally my friend's mother, a practical Punjabi lady, asked: 'How did you lose your money?' She kept hers knotted in the end of her sari, and firmly believed that people who kept their money in easily snatched handbags and wallets were asking for trouble.

'I haven't lost anything,' I said.

'Aren't the buses running?'

'Oh, the buses are running. One nearly ran over me.'

'Then why did you walk?'

'I thought I'd see more that way.'

The rest of the story is told in my journal.

The consensus of opinion in my friend's house is that I am a little mad. They have never heard of anyone in Delhi walking from choice. They prefer to wait long periods for overcrowded buses and hang on by their eyebrows, even if the distance to be covered is only a furlong. As in big cities the world over, the people of Delhi are rapidly losing the use of their legs.

I suppose Delhi is one of the least attractive cities in which to walk about. Crossing roads can be hazardous. Single and double-decker buses (many emitting smokescreens of diesel fumes), wildly driven taxis, unpredictable scooter-rickshaws, slow-moving cars and tongas, and thousands of wavering, wayward cyclists, make for chaos on the streets. On the main roads the traffic is fast and furious, and cyclists are frequently knocked over and killed. But Delhi has an acute transport problem, and the cycle is the poor man's only guarantee of getting to work in time. He cannot afford a scooter, and he cannot wait for a bus. And yet, in this city bursting with the Punjabi nouveau riche there are thousands who do have their own scooters and cars, and the number and variety of vehicles on the road increase at an alarming rate.

Setting out on another long walk, I realized that the pavement is meant for almost every purpose except walking. I am on the Najafgarh Road, heading in the general direction of central Delhi. It is a straight road, but this is no straight walk. To find a thirty-yard stretch of unoccupied pavement is most unlikely. In a territory where every square foot of land has a high price, why should so much good pavement go to waste?

The first two wayside stalls belong to sellers of lottery tickets. Theirs is a thriving business. All over Delhi, at almost every street corner, there is someone selling lottery tickets. The prizes are attractive enough. The owner of the winning ticket collects ₹250,000—sometimes more—and there are a number of other prizes. And the income accruing to the state is also tremendous—so much so that almost every state in the country, including Delhi, has climbed on the lottery bandwagon. After all, it is easier than collecting taxes. No one, not even the street sweeper, grudges giving a rupee to the government if there is a chance in a million of his winning a fortune.

While the poor man is quite willing to part with his rupee, it is the rich man, the thriving businessman, who often goes in for lottery tickets in a big way, sometimes buying up forty or fifty tickets at a time. He believes that while it is great to be rich, there is nothing like getting richer.

How times have changed. Ten years ago, if I asked a Sikh boy what he would like to be on growing up, he would unhesitatingly have said, 'I'll join the Army'—or the Navy, or the Air Force. He was proud of his martial traditions. Yesterday, while talking to an intelligent twelve-year-old Sikh, I asked the same question, and received this reply: 'I'll open a cinema, or deal in spare parts.'

No spirit of adventure, no vision of faraway places—unless it be of a cloth shop in Bangkok! The boy confessed that what he really wanted in life was a television set bigger and better than his neighbour's.

But Delhi is not entirely Punjabi. Here on the Najafgarh Road I find a community of Lohiawalas, a gypsy tribe of blacksmiths who have wandered into Delhi, camped on the pavement, and gone about their ancient and traditional way of living, supremely indifferent to the fast pace, the noise of traffic, the neon signs and Western clothes that surround them on all sides. Their bullock-carts (in which they travel and sleep and live and die and have their babies) stand just off the pavement; these are lined with old iron, stamped with decorative patterns and studded with coloured stones.

A charcoal fire has been made in a hole in the ground, and this is kept alive by a bellows worked by a wheel turned by an attractive woman wearing a black blouse and black skirt. This sombre attire is set off by heavy silver anklets and a pair of very lively eyes. Another pair of bellows has been fashioned out of goat's skin. A man is beating out a strip of red-hot tin on his anvil. A boy is filling a bent bicycle-pump with sand (to keep it firm) before straightening it out with his hammer. The entire family, including bearded old men, wizened old women ready to take off on broomsticks, and naked grandchildren, is at work. Handsome people these; and although they live in dirt and squalor, they seem quiet and dignified.

A little farther along the road are some people making what appear to be straw mats. These turn out to be roofs for the small shacks belonging to the Rajasthani labourers who live on the other side of an open drain. The walls of these shacks are about four feet high, the rooms about six feet square. There is no sanitation. People use the drain. They bathe at a public tap. During the rains, water moves sluggishly along this drain, but now it is dry except for pools of stagnant, slimy water, a grey liquid tinged with green. It must hold treasures for anyone searching for biological specimens. (And indeed, the enterprising Delhiwala has not ignored this possibility, for farther along, on Link Road, frogs are on sale to biology students.)

At this side of the road lies a dead pony, knocked down at night by a speeding truck. A portion has been eaten away by dogs and jackals. It is now being pecked at by crows; when these birds tire of the stinking carcass they move on to a nearby fruit stall. No one seems to notice this, least of all the fruit vendors. Well-dressed people pass by without a glance at the dead horse or the open drain. Is it apathy, or is it that Delhi people—city people—are unobservant by nature? Does city life dull the perceptions? Are the giant cinema hoardings so overpowering, so dazzling, that everything else pales into insignificance beside them?

Some of the shack-dwellers have tried to make their homes attractive. They have whitewashed their walls, adorned them with crude but colourful drawings of birds and animals. But what a contrast there is between these humble homes and the elegant villas and bungalows of Kirti Nagar, Patel Nagar and Pusa Road, three prosperous areas of Delhi which lie on my route. A tenant has to pay anything from three to five hundred rupees a month for a small flat in one of these fine houses.

I went flat-hunting once, but I was turned away by the house-owners—not because of race, colour or religion, but because I was a bachelor. In India, staying single is something of a crime against society. Bachelors have a rough time; they seldom get invited into homes where there are girls of marriageable age.

'Are Delhi bachelors such monsters?' I asked a house agent in Rajinder Nagar.

'Most of them are very well-behaved,' he said. 'But you see, parents no longer have much confidence in their daughters. A girl sees too many films, and then she wants to have a tragic affair with the first good-looking male who comes along.'

It has taken me two hours of foot-slogging to reach Connaught Place, which is still the premier shopping centre of New Delhi, I remember it well from my childhood, in the war years, when my father was stationed at Air Headquarters in New Delhi. The capital was a small, sparsely populated town in those days. We lived in temporary RAF hutments on Wellesley Road. A multi-storeyed hotel now occupies the site. The jungle where I hunted rabbits has long since been cleared to make way for the expensive residential area of Sunder Nagar. But the central vista, leading from India Gate up to Lutyens's complex of Parliament House and the President's Estate, is still a lovely stretch of green grass, still water and shady jamun trees.

Connaught Place has not changed much. The milk bar I frequented as a boy is still there, although they do not sell milk any more; now it is espresso coffee and hamburgers. The Regal cinema has switched over to Hindi films. In its cellar is a discotheque. Shopfronts are more flashy, but service-lanes have not altered. And of course the faces and clothes are different. The British uniforms of the war years have given way to the uniforms of the hippies, who slouch about in beads and togas, unaccepted and even scorned by the local citizens. Indians are not impressed by people who do not dress well. Their concept of the true Englishman is of the sahib who dresses for dinner even when there is no dinner; they *like* that kind of Englishman. No one is as clothes-conscious as a Punjabi. He likes his shoes polished, his shirt pressed, his suit spotless—a difficult business in Delhi, where the dust, even in winter, is as thick as in the time of Emperor Shah Jahan who, proud of his new capital, asked the Persian Ambassador how it compared with his Isphahan, and received the double-edged reply: 'By God! Isphahan cannot be compared with the dust of your Delhi!'

But Shah Jahan's Delhi, the old walled city near the Yamuna, is not on my route today. I am tired and hungry, and I lunch at a dhaba, a cheap eating-house, one of many lining the outer pavements round Connaught Place. If one does not mind the filthy surroundings, there is good meat to be had in these little restaurants, most of them run by Punjabis who learned their cooking in Lahore. Certainly the food here is better and cheaper than the watered-down dishes served in some of the smart restaurants in the inner circle. The dish-washers and servers are barefooted hill boys, working in the city because their small fields in the hills do not provide a sufficient living for their families. They work quite cheerfully (for they are cheerful by nature), in spite of hard words, cuffs, and meagre wages.

Outside, on the road, a small crowd has gathered round a turbaned Pathan. For a moment I fear violence for this exotic stranger; then I realize that the crowd is merely curious, even in good humour. The Pathan is extolling the virtues of an aphrodisiac mixture which he is trying to sell. 'Be happy!' he cries. 'And make your bulbul happy!'

In spite of the family planning hoarding directly behind him, he appears to be doing good business. It is, after all, the wedding season.

I am forcibly reminded of this on my way home in the evening. The roads in and out of every residential area are blocked by shamianas put up for wedding receptions. This is illegal, but the fine is a small one, and when a father is spending thousands on his daughter's wedding, he dosen't mind paying a fine of forty rupees. He accepts the summons with good humour, and carries on with the reception. This is the month most propitious for marriages. After 15 January, four months must pass before a Hindu will marry off his daughter. Astrology plays as great a part in the lives of the people here today as it did three hundred years ago when the traveller Francois Bernier observed that no one in Delhi, Hindu or Muslim, undertook any project without first consulting his astrologer. Today, matchmakers must still study the stars in their courses before pairing a boy with a girl.

Most fathers love to give their daughters a good send-off, and Delhi marriages are splendid, glittering affairs. The bridegroom traditionally arrives on a white horse, but Delhiwalas, who like being up-to-date, often use cars, jeeps, or even tractors (because of the high perch they provide).

I find myself involved in a procession on Pusa Road. It is impossible to get past the throng of people, so I must remain with them for some distance. If I choose to attend the reception, no one will turn me away. The bride's people will be under the impression that I am one of the bridegroom's guests, and the bridegroom's group will feel sure that I belong to the bride's party. As most of the guests are seeing each other for the first time, it is possible for any well-dressed person to join the festivities. This frequently happens.

There has, of course, to be a band, and bands are chosen mainly on the strength of the volume of noise they are able to produce and sustain. A trumpet, sounding a foot away from my ear, sends me reeling to the rear of the procession. Drums, bugles, clarinets and saxophones burst into a great profanity of sound. It is not Indian music they play, but a combination of military marches and popular Hindi film tunes. There is nothing like it anywhere else on earth.

The bandsmen wear red coats and white spats, but shoes are optional. On their heads they wear what appear to be Salvation Army caps. They will play on their instruments (often independently of each other) for as long as they are paid to play, and must deliver a final burst at daybreak when the bride leaves her father's house.

It is a colourful procession, headed by small urchin boys carrying gas lamps. After them comes the band; then the bridegroom's beautifully clothed friends and relatives; and finally the bridegroom, enthroned on top of a gaily caparisoned jeep.

I take a side road and leave the procession, but find my way blocked by another marriage party. This time a heavily-built Sikh, slightly tipsy, embraces me as a long-lost brother.

He seems to know me. Quite possibly I knew him when he was a smooth-cheeked lad of fifteen; but now, disguised by a magnificent beard, he reminds me of no one I have ever known. But he wants me to join his party, and so, to humour him, I accompany him for about a hundred yards, when he suddenly forgets me and rushes off to some other old acquaintance.

I have to reconnoitre another three processions, and four more shamianas, before I reach Rajouri Garden. I keep going by eating boiled eggs. These are sold on the roadside, and the egg-seller will even peel the egg for you, and serve it sliced, with pepper and salt, on a piece of newspaper. Unfortunately all the egg-sellers disappear when summer comes, because people believe that eggs are 'heating' and should only be eaten during the winter months. I suppose the same reasoning applies to the Pathan's tonic mixture. I am almost home. It does not look as though anyone in Delhi sleeps at night, but I am ready for bed, and all the brass bands in the city (and there must be over a hundred of them) will not keep me from sleeping.

But there is something I must do first.

The seller of lottery tickets has been staring hopefully at me, and I hate to disappoint him last thing at night. So I produce a rupee and buy a ticket; and, in doing so, I feel that I have finally identified myself with the good people of Delhi.

The Last Time I Saw Delhi

I'd had this old and faded negative with me for a number of years and had never bothered to make a print from it. It was a picture of my maternal grandparents. I remembered my grandmother quite well, because a large part of my childhood had been spent in her house in Dehra after she had been widowed; but although everyone said she was fond of me, I remembered her as a stern, somewhat aloof person, of whom I was a little afraid.

I hadn't kept many family pictures and this negative was yellow and spotted with damp.

Then last week, when I was visiting my mother in hospital in Delhi, while she awaited her operation, we got talking about my grandparents, and I remembered the negative and decided I'd make a print for my mother.

When I got the photograph and saw my grandmother's face for the first time in twenty-five years, I was immediately struck by my resemblance to her. I have, like her, lived a rather spartan life, happy with my one room, just as she was content to live in a room of her own while the rest of the family took over the house! And like her, I have lived tidily. But I did not know the physical resemblance was so close—the fair hair, the heavy build, the wide forehead. She looks more like me than my mother!

In the photograph she is seated on her favourite chair, at the top of the verandah steps, and Grandfather stands behind her in the shadows thrown by a large mango tree which is not in the picture. I can tell it was a mango tree because of the pattern the leaves make on the wall. Grandfather was a slim, trim man, with a drooping moustache that was fashionable in the 1920s. By all accounts he had a mischievous sense of humour, although he looks unwell in the picture. He appears to have been quite swarthy. No wonder he was so successful in dressing up 'native' style and passing himself off as a street vendor. My mother tells me he even took my grandmother in on one occasion, and sold her a basketful of bad oranges. His character was in strong contrast to my grandmother's rather forbidding personality and Victorian sense of propriety; but they made a good match.

So here's the picture, and I am taking it to show it to my mother who lies in the Lady Hardinge Hospital, awaiting the removal of her left breast.

It is early August and the day is hot and sultry. It rained during the night, but now the sun is out and the sweat oozes through my shirt as I sit in the back of a stuffy little taxi taking me through the suburbs of Greater New Delhi.

On either side of the road are the houses of well-to-do Punjabis who came to Delhi as refugees in 1947 and now make up more than half the capital's population. Industrious, flashy, go-ahead people. Thirty years ago, fields extended on either side of this road as far as the eye could see. The Ridge, an outcrop of the Aravallis, was scrub jungle, in which the black buck roamed. Feroz Shah's fourteenth century hunting lodge stood here in splendid isolation. It is still here, hidden by petrol pumps and lost in the sounds of buses, cars, trucks and scooter rickshaws. The peacock has fled the forest, the black buck is extinct. Only the jackal remains. When, a thousand years from now, the last human has left this contaminated planet for some other star, the jackal and the crow will remain, to survive for years on all the refuse we leave behind.

It is difficult to find the right entrance to the hospital, because for about a mile along the Panchkuian Road the pavement has been obliterated by tea shops, furniture shops, and piles of accumulated junk. A public hydrant stands near the gate, and dirty water runs across the road.

I find my mother in a small ward. It is a cool, dark room, and a ceiling fan whirrs pleasantly overhead. A nurse—a dark, pretty girl from the South—is attending to my mother. She says, 'In a minute,' and proceeds to make an entry on a chart.

My mother gives me a wan smile and beckons me to come nearer. Her cheeks are slightly flushed, possibly due to fever, otherwise she looks her normal self. I find it hard to believe that the operation she will have tomorrow will only give her, at the most, another year's lease on life.

I sit at the foot of her bed. This is my third visit since I flew back from Jersey, using up all my savings in the process; and I will leave after the operation, not to fly away again, but to return to the hills which have always called me back.

'How do you feel?' I ask.

'All right. They say they will operate in the morning. They've stopped my smoking.'

'Can you drink? Your rum, I mean?'

'No. Not until a few days after the operation.'

She has a fair amount of grey in her hair, natural enough

at fifty-four. Otherwise she hasn't changed much; the same small chin and mouth, lively brown eyes. Her father's face, not her mother's.

The nurse has left us. I produce the photograph and hand it to my mother.

'The negative was lying with me all these years. I had it printed yesterday.'

'I can't see without my glasses.'

The glasses are lying on the locker near her bed. I hand them to her. She puts them on and studies the photograph.

'Your grandmother was always very fond of you.'

'It was hard to tell. She wasn't a soft woman.'

'It was her money that got you to Jersey, when you finished school. It wasn't much, just enough for the ticket.'

'I didn't know that.'

'The only person who ever left you anything. I'm afraid I've nothing to leave you, either.'

'You know very well that I've never cared a damn about money. My father taught me to write. That was inheritance enough.'

'And what did I teach you?'

'I'm not sure... Perhaps you taught me how to enjoy myself now and then.'

She looked pleased at this. 'Yes, I've enjoyed myself between troubles. But your father didn't know how to enjoy himself. That's why we quarrelled so much. And finally separated.'

'He was much older than you.'

'You've always blamed me for leaving him, haven't you?'

'I was very small at the time. You left us suddenly. My father had to look after me, and it wasn't easy for him. He was very sick. Naturally I blamed you.'

'He wouldn't let me take you away.'

'Because you were going to marry someone else.'

I break off; we have been over this before. I am not here as my father's advocate, and the time for recrimination has passed.

And now it is raining outside, and the scent of wet earth comes through the open doors, overpowering the odour of medicines and disinfectants. The dark-eyed nurse comes in again and informs me that the doctor will soon be on his rounds. I can come again in the evening, or early morning before the operation.

'Come in the evening,' says my mother. 'The others will be here then.'

'I haven't come to see the others.'

'They are looking forward to seeing you.' 'They' being my stepfather and half-brothers.

'I'll be seeing them in the morning.'

'As you like...'

And then I am on the road again, standing on the pavement, on the fringe of a chaotic rush of traffic, in which it appears that every vehicle is doing its best to overtake its neighbour. The blare of horns can be heard in the corridors of the hospital, but everyone is conditioned to the noise and pays no attention to it. Rather, the sick and the dying are heartened by the thought that people are still well enough to feel reckless, indifferent to each other's safety! In Delhi there is a feverish desire to be first in line, the first to get anything... This is probably because no one ever gets round to dealing with second-comers.

When I hail a scooter rickshaw and it stops a short distance away, someone elbows his way past me and gets in first. This epitomizes the philosophy and outlook of the Delhiwala.

So I stand on the pavement waiting for another rickshaw, which doesn't come. In Delhi, to be second in the race is to be last.

I walk all the way back to my small hotel, with a foreboding of having seen my mother for the last time.

Coming Home to Dehra

The faint queasiness I always feel towards the end of a journey probably has its origin in that first homecoming after my father's death.

It was the winter of 1944—yes, a long time ago—and the train was running through the thick sal forests near Dehra, bringing me at every click of the rails nearer to the mother I hadn't seen for four years and the stepfather I had seen just once or twice before my parents were divorced.

I was eleven and I was coming home to Dehra.

Three years earlier, after the separation, I had gone to live with my father. We were very happy together. He was serving in the RAF, at New Delhi, and we lived in a large tent somewhere near Humayun's Tomb. The area is now a very busy part of urban Delhi, but in those days it was still a wilderness of scrub jungle where black buck and nilgai roamed freely. We took long walks together, exploring the ruins of old tombs and forts; went to the pictures (George Formby comedies were special favourites of mine); collected stamps; bought books (my father had taught me to read and write before I started going to school); and made plans for going to England when the war was over.

Six months of bliss, even though it was summer and there weren't any fans, only a thick khus reed curtain which had to be splashed with water every hour by a bhisti who did the rounds of similar tents with his goat-skin water bag. I remember the tender, refreshing fragrance of the khus, and also the smell of damp earth outside, where the water had spilt.

A happy time. But it had to end. My father's periodic bouts of malarial fever resulted in his having to enter hospital for a week. The bhisti's small son came to stay with me at night, and during the day I took my meals with an Anglo-Indian family across the road.

I would have been quite happy to continue with this arrangement whenever my father was absent, but someone at air headquarters must have advised him to put me in a boarding school.

Reluctantly, he came to the decision that it would be the best thing—'until the war is over'—and in June 1943 he took me to Simla, where I was incarcerated in a preparatory school for boys.

This is not the story of my life at a boarding school. It might easily have been a public school in England; it did in fact pride itself on being the 'Eton of the East'. The traditions such as ragging and flogging, compulsory games and chapel attendance, prefects larger than life, and honour boards for everything from school captaincy to choir membership—had all apparently been borrowed from *Tom Brown's Schooldays.*

My father wrote to me regularly, and his letters were the things I looked forward to more than anything else. I went to him for the winter holidays, and the following summer he came to Simla during my mid-term break and took me out for the duration of the holidays. We stayed in a hotel called Craig-Dhu, on a spur north of Jacko Hill. It was an idyllic week—long walks, stories about phantom rickshaws, ice creams in the sun, browsings in bookshops, more plans: 'We will go to England next year.'

School seemed a stupid and heartless place after my father had gone away. He had been transferred to Calcutta and he wasn't keeping well there. Malaria again. And then jaundice. But his last letter sounded quite cheerful. He'd been selling part of his valuable stamp collection so as to have enough money for the fares to England.

One day my class teacher sent for me.

'I want to talk to you, Bond,' he said. 'Let's go for a walk.'

I knew immediately that something was wrong.

We took the path that went through the deodar forest, past Council Rock where scout meetings were held. As soon as my unfortunate teacher (no doubt cursing the headmaster for having given him this unpleasant task) started on the theme of 'God wanting your father in a higher and better place,' as though there could be any better place than Jacko Hill in mid-summer, I knew my father was dead, and burst into tears.

They let me stay in the school hospital for a few days until I felt better. The headmaster visited me there and took away the pile of my father's letters that I'd kept beside me.

'Your father's letters. You might lose them. Why not leave them with me? Then at the end of the year, before you go home, you can come and collect them.'

Unwillingly I gave him the letters. He told me he'd heard from my mother that I would be going home to her at the end of the year. He seemed surprised that I evinced no interest in this prospect.

At the end of the year, the day before school closed, I went to the headmaster's office and asked for my letters.

'What letters?' he said. His desk was piled with papers

and correspondence, and he was irritated by my interruption.

'My father's letters,' I explained. 'I gave them to you to keep for me, Sir—when he died...'

'Letters. Are you sure you gave them to me?'

He grew more irritated. 'You must be mistaken, Bond. Why should I want to keep your father's letters?'

'I don't know, Sir. You said I could collect them before going home.'

'Look, I don't remember any letters and I'm very busy just now, so run along. I'm sure you're mistaken, but if I find your letters, I'll send them to you.'

I don't suppose he meant to be unkind, but he was the first man who aroused in me feelings of hate...

As the train drew into Dehra. I looked out of the window to see if there was anyone on the platform waiting to receive me. The station was crowded enough, as most railway stations are in India, with overloaded travellers, shouting coolies, stray dogs, stray stationmasters... Pandemonium broke loose as the train came to a halt and people debauched from the carriages. I was thrust on the platform with my tin trunk and small attaché case. I sat on the trunk and waited for someone to find me.

Slowly the crowd melted away. I was left with one elderly coolie who was too feeble to carry heavy luggage and had decided that my trunk was just the right size and weight for his head and shoulders. I waited another ten minutes, but no representative of my mother or stepfather appeared. I permitted the coolie to lead me out of the station to the tonga stand.

Those were the days when everyone, including high-ranking officials, went about in tongas. Dehra had just one taxi. I was quite happy sitting beside a rather smelly, paan-spitting tonga driver, while his weary, underfed pony clip-clopped along the quiet tree-lined roads.

Dehra was always a good place for trees. The valley soil is very fertile, the rainfall fairly heavy; almost everything grows there, if given the chance. The roads were lined with neem and mango trees, eucalyptus, Persian lilac, jacaranda, amaltas (laburnum) and many others. In the gardens of the bungalows were mangoes, litchis and guavas; sometimes jackfruit and papaya. I did not notice all these trees at once; I came to know them as time passed.

The tonga first took me to my grandmother's house. I was under the impression that my mother still lived there.

A lovely, comfortable bungalow that spread itself about the grounds in an easy-going, old-fashioned way. There was even smoke coming from the chimneys, reminding me of the smoke from my grandfather's pipe. When I was eight, I had spent several months there with my grandparents. In retrospect it had been an idyllic interlude. But Grandfather was dead. Grandmother lived alone.

White-haired, but still broad in the face and even broader behind, she was astonished to see me getting down from the tonga.

'Didn't anyone meet you at the station?' she asked.

I shook my head. Grandmother said: 'Your mother doesn't live here any more. You can come in and wait, but she may be worried about you, so I'd better take you to her place. Come on, help me up into the tonga… I might have known it would be a white horse. It always makes me nervous sitting in a tonga behind a white horse.'

'Why, Granny?'

'I don't know, I suppose white horses are nervous, too. Anyway, they are always trying to topple me out. Not so fast, driver!' she called out, as the tonga man cracked his whip and the pony changed from a slow shuffle to a brisk trot.

It took us about twenty-five minutes to reach my stepfather's house which was in the Dalanwala area, not far from the dry bed of the seasonal Rispana river. My grandmother, seeing that I was in need of moral support, got down with me, while the tonga driver carried my bedding roll and tin trunk on to the verandah. The front door was bolted from inside. We had to knock on it repeatedly and call out before it was opened by a servant who did not look pleased at being disturbed. When he saw my grandmother he gave her a deferential salaam, then gazed at me with open curiosity.

'Where's the Memsahib?' asked grandmother. 'Out,' said the servant.

'I can see that but where have they gone?'

'They went yesterday to Motichur, for shikar. They will be back this evening.'

Grandmother looked upset, but motioned to the servant to bring in my things. 'Weren't they expecting the boy?' she asked. 'Yes,' he said looking at me again. 'But they said he would be arriving tomorrow.'

'They'd forgotten the date,' said Grandmother in a huff. 'Anyway, you can unpack and have a wash and change your clothes.'

Turning to the servant, she asked, 'Is there any lunch?'

'I will make lunch,' he said. He was staring at me again, and I felt uneasy with his eyes on me. He was tall and swarthy, with oily, jet-black hair and a thick moustache. A heavy scar ran down his left cheek, giving him a rather sinister appearance. He wore a torn shirt and dirty pyjamas. His broad, heavy feet were wet. They left marks on the uncarpeted floor.

A baby was crying in the next room, and presently a woman (who turned out to be the cook's wife) appeared in the doorway, jogging the child in her arms.

'They've left the baby behind, too,' said Grandmother, becoming more and more irate. 'He is your young brother. Only six months old.' I hadn't been told anything about a younger brother. The discovery that I had one came as something of a shock. I wasn't prepared for a baby brother, least of all a baby half-brother. I examined the child without much enthusiasm. He looked healthy enough and he cried with gusto.

'He's a beautiful baby,' said Grandmother. 'Well, I've got work to do. The servants will look after you. You can come and see me in a day or two. You've grown since I last saw you. And you're getting pimples.'

This reference to my appearance did not displease me as Grandmother never indulged in praise. For her to have observed my pimples indicated that she was fond of me.

The tonga driver was waiting for her. 'I suppose I'll have to use the same tonga,' she said. 'Whenever I need a tonga, they disappear, except for the ones with white ponies... When your mother gets back, tell her I want to see her. Shikar, indeed. An infant to look after, and they've gone shooting.'

Grandmother settled herself in the tonga, nodded in response to the cook's salaam, and took a tight grip of the armrests of her seat. The driver flourished his whip and the pony set off at the same listless, unhurried trot, while my grandmother, feeling quite certain that she was going to be hurtled to her doom by a wild white pony, set her teeth and clung tenaciously to the tonga seat. I was sorry to see her go.

My mother and stepfather returned in the evening from their hunting trip with a pheasant which was duly handed over to the cook, whose name was Mangal Singh. My mother gave me a perfunctory kiss. I think she was pleased to see me, but I was accustomed to a more intimate caress from my father, and the strange reception I had received made me realize the extent of my loss. Boarding school life had been routine. Going home was something that I had always looked forward to. But going home had meant my father, and now he had vanished and I was left quite desolate.

I suppose if one is present when a loved one dies, or sees him dead and laid out and later buried, one is convinced of the finality of the thing and finds it easier to adapt to the changed circumstances. But when you hear of a death, a father's death, and have only the faintest idea of the manner of his dying, it is rather a lot for the imagination to cope with—especially when the imagination is a small boy's. There being no tangible evidence of my father's death, it was, for me, not a death but a disappearance. And although this enabled me to remember him as a living, smiling, breathing person, it meant that I was not wholly reconciled to his death, and subconsciously expected him to turn up (as he often did, when I most needed him) and deliver me from any unpleasant situation.

My stepfather barely noticed me. The first thing he did on coming into the house was to pour himself a whisky and soda. My mother, after inspecting the baby, did likewise. I was left to unpack and settle in my room.

I was fortunate in having my own room. I was as desirous of my own privacy as much as my mother and stepfather were desirous of theirs. My stepfather, a local businessman, was ready to put up with me provided I did not get in the way. And, in a different way, I was ready to put up with him, provided he left me alone. I was even willing that my mother should leave me alone.

There was a big window in my room, and I opened it to the evening breeze, and gazed out on to the garden, a rather unkempt place where marigolds and a sort of wild blue everlasting grew rampant among the litchi trees.

The Eyes Have It

I had the train compartment to myself up to Rohana, then a girl got in. The couple who saw her off was probably her parents. They seemed very anxious about her comfort and the woman gave the girl detailed instructions as to where to keep her things, when not to lean out of windows and how to avoid speaking to strangers.

They called their goodbyes and the train pulled out of the station. As I was totally blind at the time, my eyes sensitive only to light and darkness, I was unable to tell what the girl looked like. But I knew she wore slippers from the way they slapped against her heels.

It would take me some time to discover something about her looks and perhaps I never would. But I liked the sound of her voice and even the sound of her slippers.

'Are you going all the way to Dehra?' I asked. I must have been sitting in a dark corner because my voice startled her. She gave a little exclamation and said, 'I didn't know anyone else was here.'

Well, it often happens that people with good eyesight fail to see what is right in front of them. They have too much to take in, I suppose. Whereas people who cannot see (or see very little) have to take in only the essentials, whatever registers tellingly on their remaining senses.

'I didn't see you either,' I said. 'But I heard you come in.'

I wondered if I would be able to prevent her from discovering that I was blind. Provided I keep to my seat, I thought, it shouldn't be too difficult.

The girl said, 'I'm getting off at Saharanpur. My aunt is meeting me there.'

'Then I had better not get too familiar,' I replied. 'Aunts are usually formidable creatures.'

'Where are you going?' she asked. 'To Dehra and then to Mussoorie.'

'Oh, how lucky you are. I wish I was going to Mussoorie. I love the hills. Especially in October.'

'Yes, this is the best time,' I said, calling on my memories. 'The hills are covered with wild dahlias, the sun is delicious, and at night you can sit in front of a log fire and drink a little brandy. Most of the tourists have gone and the roads are quiet and almost deserted. Yes, October is the best time.'

She was silent. I wondered if my words had touched her or whether she thought me a romantic fool. Then I made a mistake.

'What is it like outside?' I asked.

She seemed to find nothing strange in the question. Had she noticed already that I could not see? But her next question removed my doubts.

'Why don't you look out of the window?' she asked.

I moved easily along the berth and felt for the window ledge. The window was open and I faced it, making a pretence of studying the landscape. I heard the panting of the engine, the rumble of the wheels, and, in my mind's eye I could see telegraph posts flashing by.

'Have you noticed,' I ventured, 'that the trees seem to be moving while we seem to be standing still?'

'That always happens,' she said. 'Do you see any animals?'

'No,' I answered quite confidently. I knew that there were hardly any animals left in the forests near Dehra. I turned from the window and faced the girl, and for a while we sat in silence.

'You have an interesting face,' I remarked. I was becoming quite daring but it was a safe remark. Few girls can resist flattery. She laughed pleasantly—a clear, ringing laugh.

'It's nice to be told I have an interesting face. I'm tired of people telling me I have a pretty face.'

Oh, so you do have a pretty face, thought I. And aloud I said, 'Well, an interesting face can also be pretty.'

'You are a very gallant young man,' she said. 'But why are you so serious?'

I thought, then, that I would try to laugh for her, but the thought of laughter only made me feel troubled and lonely.

'We'll soon be at your station,' I said.

'Thank goodness it's a short journey. I can't bear to sit in a train for more than two or three hours.'

Yet, I was prepared to sit there for almost any length of time, just to listen to her talk. Her voice had the sparkle of a mountain stream. As soon as she left the train she would forget our brief encounter. But it would stay with me for the rest of the journey and for some time after.

The engine's whistle shrieked, the carriage wheels changed their sound and rhythm, the girl got up and began to collect her things.

I wondered if she wore her hair in a bun or if it was plaited. Perhaps it was hanging loose over her shoulders. Or was it cut very short?

The train drew slowly into the station. Outside, there was

the shouting of porters and vendors and a high-pitched female voice near the carriage door. That voice must have belonged to the girl's aunt.

'Goodbye,' the girl said.

She was standing very close to me. So close that the perfume from her hair was tantalizing. I wanted to raise my hand and touch her hair but she moved away. Only the scent of perfume still lingered where she had stood.

There was some confusion in the doorway. A man, getting into the compartment, stammered an apology. Then the door banged and the world was shut out again. I returned to my berth. The guard blew his whistle and we moved off. Once again I had a game to play and a new fellow traveller.

The train gathered speed, the wheels took up their song, the carriage groaned and shook. I found the window and sat in front of it, staring into the daylight that was darkness for me.

So many things were happening outside the window. It could be a fascinating game guessing what went on out there.

The man who had entered the compartment broke into my reverie.

'You must be disappointed,' he said. 'I'm not nearly as attractive a travelling companion as the one who just left.'

'She was an interesting girl,' I said. 'Can you tell me—did she keep her hair long or short?'

'I don't remember,' he said sounding puzzled. 'It was her eyes I noticed, not her hair. She had beautiful eyes but they were of no use to her. She was completely blind. Didn't you notice?'

My Father's Trees in Dehra

Our trees still grow in Dehra. This is one part of the world where trees are a match for man. An old peepul may be cut down to make way for a new building; two peepul trees will sprout from the walls of the building. In Dehra the air is moist, the soil hospitable to seeds and probing roots. The valley of Dehra Dun lies between the first range of the Himalayas and the smaller but older Siwalik range. Dehra is an old town, but it was not in the reign of Rajput princes or Mogul kings that it really grew and flourished; it acquired a certain size and importance with the coming of British and Anglo-Indian settlers. The English have an affinity with trees, and in the rolling hills of Dehra they discovered a retreat which, in spite of snakes and mosquitoes, reminded them, just a little bit, of England's green and pleasant land.

The mountains to the north are austere and inhospitable; the plains to the south are flat, dry and dusty. But Dehra is green. I look out of the train window at daybreak to see the sal and shisham trees sweep by majestically, while trailing vines and great clumps of bamboo give the forest a darkness and density which add to its mystery. There are still a few tigers in these forests; only a few, and perhaps they will survive, to stalk the spotted deer and drink at forest pools.

I grew up in Dehra. My grandfather built a bungalow on the outskirts of the town at the turn of the century. The house was sold a few years after Independence. No one knows me now in Dehra, for it is over twenty years since I left the place, and my boyhood friends are scattered and lost. And although the India of Kim is no more, and the Grand Trunk Road is now a procession of trucks instead of a slow-moving caravan of horses and camels, India is still a country in which people are easily lost and quickly forgotten.

From the station I can take either a taxi or a snappy little scooter rickshaw (Dehra had neither before 1950), but, because I am on an unashamedly sentimental pilgrimage, I take a tonga, drawn by a lean, listless pony, and driven by a tubercular old Muslim in a shabby green waistcoat. Only two or three tongas stand outside the station. There were always twenty or thirty here in the 1940s when I came home from boarding school to be met at the station by my grandfather; but the days of the tonga are nearly over, and in many ways this is a good thing, because most tonga ponies are overworked and underfed. Its wheels squeaking from lack of oil and its seat slipping out from under me, the tonga drags me through the bazaars of Dehra. A couple of miles of this slow, funereal pace makes me impatient to use my own legs, and I dismiss the tonga when we get to the small Dilaram Bazaar.

It is a good place from which to start walking.

The Dilaram Bazaar has not changed very much. The shops are run by a new generation of bakers, barbers and banias, but professions have not changed. The cobblers belong to the lower castes, the bakers are Muslims, the tailors are Sikhs. Boys still fly kites from the flat rooftops, and women wash clothes on the canal steps. The canal comes down from Rajpur and goes underground here, to emerge about a mile away.

I have to walk only a furlong to reach my grandfather's house. The road is lined with eucalyptus, jacaranda and laburnum trees. In the compounds there are small groves of mangoes, litchis and papayas. The poinsettia thrusts its scarlet leaves over garden walls. Every verandah has its bougainvillea creeper, every garden its bed of marigolds. Potted palms, those symbols of Victorian snobbery, are popular with Indian housewives. There are a few houses, but most of the bungalows were built by 'old India hands' on their retirement from the army, the police or the railways. Most of the present owners are Indian businessmen or government officials.

I am standing outside my grandfather's house. The wall has been raised, and the wicket gate has disappeared; I cannot get a clear view of the house and garden. The nameplate identifies the owner as Major General Saigal; the house has had more than one owner since my grandparents sold it in 1949.

On the other side of the road there is an orchard of litchi trees. This is not the season for fruit, and there is no one looking after the garden. By taking a little path that goes through the orchard, I reach higher ground and gain a better view of our old house.

Grandfather built the house with granite rocks taken from the foothills. It shows no sign of age. The lawn has disappeared; but the big jackfruit tree, giving shade to the side verandah, is still there. In this tree I spent my afternoons, absorbed in my Magnets, Champions and Hotspurs, while sticky mango juice trickled down my chin. (One could not eat the jackfruit unless it was cooked into a vegetable curry.) There was a hole in the bole of the tree in which I kept my pocket knife, top, catapult and any badges or buttons that could be saved from my father's RAF tunics when he came home on leave. There was also an Iron Cross, a relic of the First World War, given to me by my grandfather. I have managed to keep the Iron Cross; but what did I do with my top and catapult? Memory fails me. Possibly they are still in the hole in the jackfruit tree; I must have forgotten to collect them when we went away after my father's death. I am seized by a whimsical urge to walk in at the gate, climb into the branches of the jackfruit tree and recover my lost possessions. What would the present owner, the major general (retired), have to say if I politely asked permission to look for a catapult left behind more than twenty years ago?

An old man is coming down the path through the litchi trees. He is not a major general but a poor street vendor. He carries a small tin trunk on his head, and walks very slowly. When he sees me, he stops and asks me if I will buy something. I can think of nothing I need, but the old man looks so tired, so very old, that I am afraid he will collapse if he moves any further along the path without resting. So I ask him to show me his wares. He cannot get the box off his head by himself, but together we manage to set it down in the shade, and the old man insists on spreading its entire contents on the grass; bangles, combs, shoelaces, safety pins, cheap stationery, buttons, pomades, elastic and scores of other household necessities.

When I refuse buttons because there is no one to sew them on for me, he piles me with safety pins. I say no; but as he moves from one article to another, his querulous, persuasive voice slowly wears down my resistance, and I end up buying envelopes, a letter pad (pink roses on bright blue paper), a one-rupee fountain pen guaranteed to leak and several yards of elastic. I have no idea what I will do with the elastic, but the old man convinces me that I cannot live without it.

Exhausted by the effort of selling me a lot of things I obviously do not want, he closes his eyes and leans back against the trunk of a litchi tree. For a moment I feel rather nervous. Is he going to die sitting here beside me? He sinks to his haunches and puts his chin on his hands. He only wants to talk.

'I am very tired, huzoor,' he says. 'Please do not mind if I sit here for a while.'

'Rest for as long as you like,' I say. 'That's a heavy load you've been carrying.'

He comes to life at the chance of a conversation and says, 'When I was a young man, it was nothing. I could carry my box up from Rajpur to Mussoorie by the bridle path—seven steep miles! But now I find it difficult to cover the distance from the station to Dilaram Bazaar.'

'Naturally. You are quite old.'

'I am seventy, sahib.'

'You look very fit for your age.' I say this to please him; he looks frail and brittle. 'Isn't there someone to help you?' I ask.

'I had a servant boy last month, but he stole my earnings and ran off to Delhi. I wish my son was alive—he would not have permitted me to work like a mule for a living—but he was killed in the riots in '47.'

'Have you no other relatives?'

'I have outlived them all. That is the curse of a healthy life. Your friends, your loved ones, all go before you, and in the end you are left alone. But I must go too, before long. The road to the bazaar seems to grow longer every day. The stones are harder. The sun is hotter in the summer, and the wind much colder in the winter. Even some of the trees that were there in my youth have grown old and have died. I have outlived the trees.'

He has outlived the trees. He is like an old tree himself,

gnarled and twisted. I have the feeling that if he falls asleep in the orchard, he will strike root here, sending out crooked branches. I can imagine a small bent tree wearing a black waistcoat; a living scarecrow.

He closes his eyes again, but goes on talking.

'The English memsahibs would buy great quantities of elastic. Today it is ribbons and bangles for the girls, and combs for the boys. But I do not make much money. Not because I cannot walk very far. How many houses do I reach in a day? Ten, fifteen. But twenty years ago I could visit more than fifty houses. That makes a difference.'

'Have you always been here?'

'Most of my life, huzoor. I was here before they built the motor road to Mussoorie. I was here when the sahibs had their own carriages and ponies and the memsahibs their own rickshaws. I was here before there were any cinemas. I was here when the Prince of Wales came to Dehra Dun… Oh, I have been here a long time, huzoor. I was here when that house was built,' he says pointing with his chin towards my grandfather's house. 'Fifty, sixty years ago it must have been. I cannot remember exactly. What is ten years when you have lived seventy? But it was a tall, red-bearded sahib who built that house. He kept many creatures as pets. A kachwa (turtle) was one of them. And there was a python, which crawled into my box one day and gave me a terrible fright. The sahib used to keep it hanging from his shoulders, like a garland. His wife, the burra mem, always bought a lot from me—lots of elastic. And there were sons, one a teacher, another in the air force, and there were always children in the house. Beautiful children. But they went away many years ago. Everyone has gone away.'

I do not tell him that I am one of the 'beautiful children'. I doubt if he will believe me. His memories are of another age, another place, and for him there are no strong bridges into the present.

'But others have come,' I say.

'True, and that is as it should be. That is not my complaint. My complaint—should God be listening—is that I have been left behind.'

He gets slowly to his feet and stands over his shabby tin box, gazing down at it with a mix of disdain and affection. I help him to lift and balance it on the flattened cloth on his head. He does not have the energy to turn and make a salutation of any kind; but, setting his sights on the distant hills, he walks down the path with steps that are shaky and slow but still wonderfully straight.

I wonder how much longer he will live. Perhaps a year or two, perhaps a week, perhaps an hour. It will be an end of living, but it will not be death. He is too old for death; he can only sleep; he can only fall gently, like an old, crumpled brown leaf.

I leave the orchard. The bend in the road hides my grandfather's house. I reach the canal again. It emerges from under a small culvert, where ferns and maidenhair grow in the shade. The water, coming from a stream in the foothills, rushes along with a familiar sound; it does not lose its momentum until the canal has left the gently sloping streets of the town.

There are new buildings on this road, but the small police station is housed in the same old lime-washed bungalow. A couple of off-duty policemen, partly uniformed but with their pyjamas on, stroll about.

I cannot forget this little police station. Nothing very exciting ever happened in its vicinity until, in 1947, communal riots broke out in Dehra. Then, bodies were regularly fished out of the canal and dumped on a growing pile in the station compound. I was only a boy, but when I looked over the wall at that pile of corpses, there was no one who paid any attention to me. They were too busy to send me away. At the same time they knew that I was perfectly safe; while Hindus and Muslims were at each other's throats, a white boy could walk the streets in safety. No one was any longer interested in the Europeans.

The people of Dehra are not violent by nature, and the town has no history of communal discord. But when refugees from the partitioned Punjab poured into Dehra in thousands, the atmosphere became charged with tension. These refugees, many of them Sikhs, had lost their homes and livelihoods; many had seen their loved ones butchered. They were in a fierce and vengeful frame of mind. The calm, sleepy atmosphere of Dehra was shattered during two months of looting and murder. The Muslims who could get away, fled. The poorer members of the community remained in a refugee camp until the holocaust was over; then they returned to their former occupations, frightened and deeply mistrustful. The old boxman was one of them.

I cross the canal and take the road that will lead me to the riverbed. This was one of my father's favourite walks. He, too, was a walking man. Often, when he was home on leave, he would say, 'Ruskin, let's go for a walk,' and we would slip off together and walk down to the riverbed or into the sugarcane fields or across the railway lines and into the jungle.

On one of those walks (this was before Independence), I remember him saying, 'After the war is over, we'll be going to England. Would you like that?'

'I don't know,' I said. 'Can't we stay in India?'

'It won't be ours any more.'

'Has it always been ours?' I asked.

'For a long time,' he said, 'over two hundred years. But we have to give it back now.'

'Give it back to whom?' I asked. I was only nine.

'To the Indians,' said my father.

The only Indians I had known till then were my ayah and the cook and the gardener and their children, and I could not imagine them wanting to be rid of us. The only other Indian who came to the house was Dr Ghose, and it was frequently said of him that he was more English than the English. I could understand my father better when he said, 'After the war, there'll be a job for me in England. There'll be nothing for me here.'

The war had at first been a distant event; but somehow it kept coming closer. My aunt, who lived in London with her two children, was killed with them during an air raid; then my father's younger brother died of dysentery on the long walk out from Burma. Both these tragic events depressed my father. Never in good health (he had been prone to attacks of malaria), he looked more worn and wasted every time he came home. His personal life was far from being happy, as he and my mother had separated, she to marry again. I think he looked forward a great deal to the days he spent with me; far more than I could have realized at the time. I was someone to come back to; someone for whom things could be planned; someone who could learn from him.

Dehra suited him. He was always happy when he was among trees, and this happiness communicated itself to me. I felt like drawing close to him. I remember sitting beside him on the verandah steps when I noticed the tendril of a creeping vine that was trailing near my feet. As we sat there, doing nothing in particular—in the best gardens, time has no meaning—I found that the tendril was moving almost imperceptibly away from me and towards my father. Twenty minutes later it had crossed the verandah steps and was touching his feet. This, in India, is the sweetest of salutations.

There is probably a scientific explanation for the plant's behaviour—something to do with the light and warmth on the verandah steps—but I like to think that its movements were motivated simply by an affection for my father. Sometimes, when I sat alone beneath a tree, I felt a little lonely or lost. As soon as my father rejoined me, the atmosphere lightened, the tree itself became more friendly.

Most of the fruit trees round the house were planted by father; but he was not content with planting trees in the garden. On rainy days we would walk beyond the riverbed, armed with cuttings and saplings, and then we would amble through the jungle, planting flowering shrubs between the sal and shisham trees.

'But no one ever comes here,' I protested the first time. 'Who is going to see them?'

'Some day,' he said, 'someone may come this way... If people keep cutting trees, instead of planting them, there'll soon be no forests left at all, and the world will be just one vast desert.' The prospect of a world without trees became a sort of nightmare for me (and one reason why I shall never want to live on the treeless moon), and I assisted my father in his tree planting with great enthusiasm.

'One day the trees will move again,' he said. 'They've been standing still for thousands of years. There was a time when they could walk about like people, but someone cast a spell on them and rooted them to one place. But they're always trying to move—see how they reach out with their arms!'

We found an island, a small rocky island in the middle of a dry riverbed. It was one of those riverbeds, so common in the foothills, which are completely dry in the summer but flooded during the monsoon rains. The rains had just begun, and the stream could still be crossed on foot, when we set out with a number of tamarind, laburnum and coral tree saplings and cuttings. We spent the day planting them on the island, then ate our lunch there, in the shelter of a wild plum.

My father went away soon after that tree planting. Three months later, in Calcutta, he died.

I was sent to boarding school. My grandparents sold the house and left Dehra. After school, I went to England. The years passed, my grandparents died, and when I returned to India I was the only member of the family in the country.

And now I am in Dehra again, on the road to the riverbed. The houses with their trim gardens are soon behind me, and I am walking through fields of flowering mustard, which make a carpet of yellow blossom stretching away towards the jungle and the foothills.

The riverbed is dry at this time of the year. A herd of skinny cattle graze on the short brown grass at the edge of the jungle. The sal trees have been thinned out. Could our trees have survived? Will our island be there, or has some flash flood during a heavy monsoon washed it away completely?

As I look across the dry watercourse, my eye is caught by the spectacular red plumes of the coral blossom. In contrast with the dry, rocky riverbed, the little island is a green oasis. I walk across to the trees and notice that a number of parrots have come to live in them. A koel challenges me with a rising *who-are-you, who-are you.*

But the trees seem to know me. They whisper among themselves and beckon me nearer. And looking around, I find that other trees and wild plants and grasses have sprung up under the protection of the trees we planted.

They have multiplied. They are moving. In this small forgotten corner of the world, my father's dreams are coming true, and the trees are moving again.

Reunion at the Regal

If you want to see a ghost, just stand outside New Delhi's Regal Cinema for twenty minutes or so. The approach to the grand old cinema hall is a great place for them. Sooner or later you'll see a familiar face in the crowd. Before you have time to recall who it was or who it may be, it will have disappeared and you will be left wondering if it really was so-and-so…because surely so-and-so died several years ago…

The Regal was very posh in the early '40s when, in the company of my father, I saw my first film there. The Connaught Place cinemas still had a new look about them, and they showed the latest offerings from Hollywood and Britain. To see a Hindi film, you had to travel all the way to Kashmere Gate or Chandni Chowk.

Over the years, I was in and out of the Regal quite a few times, and so I became used to meeting old acquaintances or glimpsing familiar faces in the foyer or on the steps outside.

On one occasion I was mistaken for a ghost.

I was about thirty at the time. I was standing on the steps of the arcade, waiting for someone, when a young Indian male came up to me and said something in German or what sounded like German.

'I'm sorry,' I said. 'I don't understand. You may speak to me in English or Hindi.'

'Aren't you Hans? We met in Frankfurt last year. You look exactly like Hans.'

'Maybe I'm his double. Or maybe I'm his ghost!'

My facetious remark did not amuse the young man. He looked confused and stepped back, a look of horror spreading over his face. 'No, no,' he stammered. 'Hans is alive, you can't be his ghost!'

'I was only joking.'

But he had turned away, hurrying off through the crowd. He seemed agitated. I shrugged philosophically. So I had a double called Hans, I reflected; perhaps I'd run into him some day.

I mention this incident only to show that most of us have lookalikes, and that sometimes we see what we want to see, or are looking for, even if on looking closer, the resemblance isn't all that striking.

But there was no mistaking Kishen when he approached me. I hadn't seen him for five or six years, but he looked much the same. Bushy eyebrows, offset by gentle eyes; a determined chin, offset by a charming smile. The girls had always liked him, and he knew it; and he was content to let them do the pursuing.

We saw a film—I think it was *The Wind Cannot Read*—and then we strolled across to the old Standard Restaurant, ordered dinner and talked about old times, while the small band played sentimental tunes from the 1950s.

Yes, we talked about old times—growing up in Dehra, where we lived next door to each other, exploring our neighbours' litchi orchards, cycling about the town in the days before the scooter had been invented, kicking a football around on the maidan, or just sitting on the compound wall doing nothing. I had just finished school, and an entire year stretched before me until it was time to go abroad. Kishen's father, a civil engineer, was under transfer orders, so Kishen, too, temporarily did not have to go to school.

He was an easy-going boy, quite content to be at a loose end in my company—I was to describe a couple of our escapades in my first novel, *The Room on the Roof*. I had literary pretensions; he was apparently without ambition although, as he grew older, he was to surprise me by his wide reading and erudition.

One day, while we were cycling along the bank of the Rajpur canal, he skidded off the path and fell into the canal with his cycle. The water was only waist-deep; but it was quite swift, and I had to jump in to help him. There was no real danger, but we had some difficulty getting the cycle out of the canal.

Later, he learnt to swim.

But that was after I'd gone away…

Convinced that my prospects would be better in England, my mother packed me off to her relatives in Jersey, and it was to be four long years before I could return to the land I truly cared for. In that time, many of my Dehra friends had left the town; it wasn't a place where you could do much after finishing school. Kishen wrote to me from Calcutta, where he was at an engineering college. Then he was off to 'study abroad'. I heard from him from time to time. He seemed happy. He had an equable temperament and got on quite well with most people. He had a girlfriend too, he told me.

'But,' he wrote, 'you're my oldest and best friend. Wherever I go, I'll always come back to see you.'

And, of course, he did. We met several times while I was living in Delhi, and once we revisited Dehra together and walked down Rajpur Road and ate tikkis and golgappas behind the clock tower. But the old familiar faces were missing. The streets were overbuilt and overcrowded, and the litchi gardens were fast disappearing. After we got back to Delhi, Kishen accepted a job in Mumbai. We kept in touch in desultory fashion, but our paths and our lives had taken different directions. He was busy nurturing his career with an engineering firm; I had retreated to the hills with radically different goals to write and be free of the burden of a 9-to-5 desk job.

Time went by, and I lost track of Kishen.

About a year ago, I was standing in the lobby of the India International Centre, when an attractive young woman in her mid-thirties came up to me and said, 'Hello, Rusty, don't you remember me? I'm Manju. I lived next to you and Kishen and Ranbir when we were children.'

I recognized her then, for she had always been a pretty girl, the 'belle' of Dehra's Astley Hall.

We sat down and talked about old times and new times, and I told her that I hadn't heard from Kishen for a few years. 'Didn't you know?' she asked. 'He died about two years ago.'

'What happened?' I was dismayed, even angry, that I hadn't heard about it. 'He couldn't have been more than thirty-eight.'

'It was an accident on a beach in Goa. A child had got into difficulties and Kishen swam out to save her. He did rescue the little girl, but when he swam ashore he had a heart attack. He died right there on the beach. It seems he had always had a weak heart. The exertion must have been too much for him.'

I was silent. I knew he'd become a fairly good swimmer, but I did not know about the heart.

'Was he married?' I asked.

'No, he was always the eligible bachelor boy.'

It had been good to see Manju again, even though she had given me sad news. She told me she was happily married, with a small son. We promised to keep in touch.

And that's the end of this tale, apart from my brief visit to Delhi last November.

I had taken a taxi to Connaught Place and decided to get down at the Regal. I stood there a while, undecided about what to do or where to go. It was almost time for a show to start, and there were a lot of people milling around.

I thought someone called my name. I looked around, and there was Kishen in the crowd.

'Kishen!' I called, and started after him.

But a stout lady climbing out of a scooter rickshaw got in my way, and by the time I had a clear view again, my old friend had disappeared.

Had I seen his lookalike, a double? Or had he kept his promise to come back to see me once more?

Great Spirits of the Trees

Explore the history and mythology of almost any Indian tree, and you will find that at some point in our civilization it has held an important place in the minds and hearts of the people of this land.

During the rains, when the neem-pods fall and are crushed underfoot, they give out a strong refreshing aroma which lingers in the air for days. This is because the neem gives out more oxygen than most trees. When the ancient herbalists held that the neem was a great purifier of the air, and that its leaves, bark and sap had medicinal qualities, they were quite right, for the neem is still used in medicine today.

From the earliest times it was connected with the gods who protect us from disease. Some castes regarded the tree as sacred to Sitala, the smallpox goddess. When children fell ill, a branch of the neem was waved over them. The tree is said to have sprung from the nectar of the gods, and people still chew the leaves as a means of purification, both spiritual and physical. The tree is also connected with the sun, as in the story of neem-barak, 'The Sun in the Neem Tree'. The sun-god invited to dinner a man of the Bairagi tribe whose rules forbade him to eat except by daylight. Dinner was late, and as darkness fell, the Bairagi feared he would have to go hungry. But Suraj Narayan, the sun-god, descended from a neem tree and continued shining till dinner was over.

Why have so many trees been held sacred, not only in India but the world over?

To early man they were objects of awe and wonder. The mystery of their growth, the movement of their leaves and branches, the way they seemed to die and then come to life again in spring, the growth of the plant from the seed, all these happenings appeared as miracles—as indeed they are! And because of the wonderful growth of a tree, people began to suppose that it was occupied by spirits, and devotion to a tree became devotion to the spirit or tree-god who occupied it. In *Puck of Pook's Hill,* Kipling wove some wonderful stories, around Puck, the tree-spirit, and the sacred trees of Old England—oak, ash and thorn: 'I came into England with Oak, Ash, and Thorn, and when Oak, Ash and Thorn are gone, I shall go too.'

Among the Gonds of Central India, before a man cut a tree he had to beg its pardon for the injury he was about to inflict on it. He would not shake a tree at night because the tree-spirit was asleep and might be disturbed. When a tree had to be felled, the Gonds would pour ghee on the stump, saying: 'Grow thou out of this, O Lord of the Forest, grow into a hundred shoots! May we grow with a thousand shoots.'

The beautiful mahua is a forest tree held sacred by a number of tribes. Early on the wedding morning, before he goes to fetch his bride, the Bagdi bridegroom goes through a mock marriage with a mahua tree. He embraces it and daubs it with vermilion, his right wrist is bound to it with thread, and after he is released from the tree the thread is used to attach a bunch of mahua leaves to his wrist.

There is a beautiful tradition connected with the sal tree. It is said that at the time of the Buddha's birth, his mother stretched out her hand to take hold of a branch of the sal and he was delivered. Sal trees are also said to have rendered homage to the Buddha at his death, letting fall on him their flowers out of season, and bending their branches to shade him.

Special respect is paid to trees growing near the graves of Muslim saints. Near the tomb of a famous saint, Musa Sohag, at Ahmedabad, there used to be a large old champa tree—perhaps it is still there—the branches of which were hung with glass bangles. Those anxious to have children came and offered bangles to the saint—the number of bangles depending on the means of the supplicant. If the saint favoured a wish, the champa tree 'snatched up the bangles and wore them on its arms'.

Another spectacular tree which has its place in our folklore is the dhak, or palasa, which gave its name to the battlefield of Plassey. It has the habit of dropping its leaves when it flowers, the upper and outer branches standing out in sprays of scarlet and orange. The flowers are sometimes used to dye the powder scattered at Holi, the spring festival; and the wood, said to contain the seed of fire, is used in lighting the Holi bonfire. Legend tells us that the sun-god aimed an arrow at earth, and that it took root and became the palasa tree.

The babul (or keekar) is not very impressive to look at but it will grow almost anywhere in the plains, and there are a number of old beliefs associated with it. For instance, you can cure fever and headache at a babul tree if you tie seven cotton threads from your left big toe to your head, and from your head to a branch of the tree. Then you must embrace the trunk seven times. Try it sometime. You will be so busy tying threads that you will forget you ever had a headache!

And there are no after-effects.

Another belief concerning the babul is that if you water it regularly for thirteen days, you acquire control over the spirit who occupies it. There is a story about a man in Saharanpur who did this, and when he died and his corpse was taken away for cremation, no sooner was his pyre lit than he got up and walked away!

In the folklore of India, the mango is the 'wish-fulfilling tree'. When you want to make a wish on a mango tree, shut your eyes and get someone to lead you to the tree; then rub mango blossoms in your hands, and make your wish. The favour granted lasts only for a year, and the charm must be performed again at the next flowering of the tree. In the spring, the young leaves and buds symbolize the darts of Manmatha, or Kamadeva, God of Love.

Another 'wishing tree', the kalp-vriksha, is an enormous old mulberry that is still cared for at Joshimath in Garhwal. It is said to be the tree beneath which the great Sankaracharya often meditated during his sojourn in the Himalayas. Judging by its girth, it might well be over a thousand years old.

Whole forests have been held sacred, such as that in Berar which was dedicated to a particular temple; no one dared to buy or cut the trees. The sacred groves near Mathura, where Lord Krishna sported as a youth, were also protected for centuries. But now, alas, even the hallowed groves are disappearing, making way for the demands of an ever-increasing population. A pity, because every human needs a tree of his own. Even if you do not worship the tree-spirit, you can love the tree.

All About My Walkabouts

All my life I've been a walking person. Up to this day, I have neither owned nor driven a car, bus, tractor, airplane, motorcycle, truck, or steamroller. Forced to make a choice I would as soon drive a steamroller, because of its slow but solid progress and unhurried finality. And also because other vehicles don't try hustling steamrollers off the road.

For a brief period in my early teens I had a bicycle, until I rode into a bullock cart and ruined my new cycle. The bullocks panicked and ran away with the cart while the furious cart driver was giving me a lecture on road sense. I have never bumped into a bullock cart while walking.

My earliest memories are of a place called Jamnagar, a small port on the west coast of India, then part of a princely state. My father was an English tutor to several young Indian princes and princesses. This was where my walking really began, because Jamnagar was full of spacious palaces, lawns and gardens. By the time I was four, I was exploring much of this territory on my own, with the result that I encountered my first snake. Instead of striking me dead as snakes are supposed to do, it allowed me to pass.

Living as it did so close to the ground, and sensitive to

every footfall, it must have known instinctively that I presented no threat, that I was just another small creature discovering the use of his legs. Envious of the snake's swift gliding movements, I went indoors and tried crawling about on my belly. But I wasn't much good at it. Legs were better.

My father's schoolroom and our own residence were located on the grounds of one of the older palaces, which was full of turrets, stairways and mysterious dark passages. Right on top of the building I discovered a glass-covered room, each pane of glass stained with a different colour. This room fascinated me, as I could, by turn, look through the panes of glass at a green or rose-pink or orange or deep indigo world. It was nice to be able to decide for oneself what colour the world should be!

My father took his duties seriously and taught me to read and write long before I started attending a regular school. However, it would be true to say that I first learned to read upside down. This happened because I would sit on a stool in front of the three princesses, watching them read and write, and so the view I had of their books was an upside-down view, I still read that way occasionally, especially when a book becomes boring.

There was no boredom in the palace grounds. We were situated in the middle of a veritable jungle of a garden, where marigolds and cosmos grew, rampant in the long grass. An old disused well was the home of countless pigeons, their gentle cooing by day contrasting with the shrill cries of the brain-fever bird (the hawk-cuckoo) at night. 'How very hot it's getting!' the bird seems to say. And then, in a rising crescendo, 'We feel it! *We feel* it! WE FEEL IT!'

Walking along a nearby beach, collecting seashells, I got into the habit of staring hard at the ground, a habit which has remained with me all my life. Apart from helping my thought processes, it also results in my picking up odd objects—coins, keys, broken bangles, marbles, pens, bits of crockery, pretty stones, feathers, ladybirds, seashells, snail-shells! Not to speak of old nails and horseshoes. Looking at my collection of miscellaneous objects picked up on these walks, my friends insist that I must be using a metal detector. But it's only because I keep my nose to the ground, like a bloodhound. Occasionally, of course, this habit results in my walking some way past my destination (if I happen to have one). And why not? It simply means discovering a new and different destination, sights and sounds that I might not have experienced had I ended my walk exactly where it was supposed to end. And I am not looking at the ground *all* the time. Sensitive like the snake to approaching footfalls, I look up from time to time to take note of the faces of passers-by, just in case they have something interesting to say.

A bird singing in a bush or tree has my immediate attention, so does any familiar flower or plant, particularly if it grows in an unusual place such as a crack in a wall or rooftop, or in a yard full of junk—where once I found a rosebush blooming on the roof of an old, abandoned Ford car.

I like to think that I invented the zigzag walk. Tiring of walking in straight lines, or on roads that led directly to a destination, I took to going off at tangents—taking sudden unfamiliar turnings, wandering down narrow alleyways, following cart tracks or paths through fields instead of the main roads, and in general making the walk as complicated as possible.

In this way I saw much more than I would normally have seen. Here a temple, there a mosque; now an old church; a railway siding; follow the railway line; here's a pond full of buffaloes, there a peacock preening itself under a tamarind tree; and now I'm in a field of mustard, and soon I'm walking along a canal bank, and the canal leads me back into the town, and I follow the line of the mango trees until I am home.

The adventure is not in arriving, it's the on-the-way experience. It is not the expected; it's the surprise. You are not choosing what you shall see in the world, but are giving the world an even chance to see you.

It's like drawing lines from star to star in the night sky, not forgetting many dim, shy, out-of-the-way stars, which are full of possibilities. The first turning to the left, the next to the right! I am still on my zigzag way, pursuing the diagonal between reason and the heart.

Picnic at Fox-Burn

In spite of the frenetic building activity in most hill stations, there are still a few ruins to be found on the outskirts—neglected old bungalows that have fallen or been pulled down, and which now provide shelter for bats, owls, stray goats, itinerant sadhus, and sometimes the restless spirits of those who once dwelt in them.

One such ruin is Fox-Burn, but I won't tell you exactly where it can be found, because I visit the place for purposes of meditation (or just plain contemplation) and I would hate to arrive there one morning to find about fifty people picnicking on the grass.

And yet it did witness a picnic of sorts the other day, when the children accompanied me to the ruin. They had heard it was haunted, and they wanted to see the ghost.

Rakesh is twelve, Mukesh is six, and Dolly is four, and they are not afraid of ghosts.

I should mention here, that before Fox-Burn became a ruin, back in the '40s, it was owned by an elderly English woman, Mrs Williams, who ran it as a boarding-house for several years. In the end, poor health forced her to give up this work, and during her final years, she lived alone in the huge house, with just a chowkidar to help. Her children, who had grown up on the property, had long since settled in faraway lands.

When Mrs Williams died, the chowkidar stayed on for some time until the property was disposed of; but he left as soon as he could. Late at night there would be a loud rapping on his door, and he would hear the old lady calling out: 'Shamsher Singh, open the door! Open the door, I say, and let me in!'

Needless to say, Shamsher Singh kept the door firmly closed. He returned to his village at the first opportunity. The hill station was going through a slump at the time, and the new owners pulled the house down and sold the roof and beams as scrap.

'What does Fox-Burn mean?' asked Rakesh, as we climbed the neglected, overgrown path to the ruin.

'Well, Burn is a Scottish word meaning stream or spring. Perhaps there was a spring here, once. If so, it dried up long ago.'

'And did a fox live here?'

'Maybe a fox came to drink at the spring. There are still foxes living on the mountain. Sometimes you can see them dancing in the moonlight.'

Passing through a gap in a wall, we came upon the ruins of the house. In the bright light of a summer morning it did not look in the least spooky or depressing. A line of Doric pillars were all that remained of what must have been an elegant porch and verandah. Beyond them, through the deodars, we could see the distant snows. It must have been a lovely spot in which to spend the better part of one's life. No wonder Mrs Williams wanted to come back.

The children were soon scampering about on the grass,

whilst I sought shelter beneath a huge chestnut tree.

There is no tree so friendly as the chestnut, especially in summer when it is in full leaf.

Mukesh discovered an empty water-tank and Rakesh suggested that it had once fed the burn that no longer existed. Dolly busied herself making nosegays with the daisies that grew wild in the grass.

Rakesh looked up suddenly. He pointed to a path on the other side of the ruin, and exclaimed: 'Look, what's that? Is it Mrs Williams?'

'A ghost!' said Mukesh excitedly.

But it turned out to be the local washerwoman, a large white bundle on her head, taking a short-cut across the property.

A more peaceful place could hardly be imagined, until a large black dog, a spaniel of sorts, arrived on the scene. He wanted someone to play with—indeed, he insisted on playing—and ran circles round us until we threw sticks for him to fetch and gave him half our sandwiches.

'Whose dog is it?' asked Rakesh.

'I've no idea.'

'Did Mrs Williams keep a black dog?'

'Is it *a ghost* dog?' asked Mukesh.

'It looks real to me', I said.

'And it's eaten all my biscuits,' said Dolly.

'Don't ghosts have to eat?' asked Mukesh.

'I don't know. We'll have to ask one.'

'It can't be any fun being a ghost if you can't eat,' declared Mukesh.

The black dog left us as suddenly as he had appeared, and as there was no sign of an owner, I began to wonder if he had not, after all, been an apparition.

A cloud came over the sun, the air grew chilly.

'Let's go home,' said Mukesh.

'I'm hungry,' said Rakesh.

'Come along, Dolly,' I called.

But Dolly couldn't be seen.

We called out to her, and looked behind trees and pillars, certain that she was hiding from us. Almost five minutes passed in searching for her, and a sick feeling of apprehension was coming over me, when Dolly emerged from the ruins and ran towards us.

'Where have you been?' we demanded, almost with one voice.

'I was playing—in there—in the old house. Hide and seek.'

'On your own?'

'No, there were two children. A boy and a girl. They were playing too.'

'I haven't seen any children,' I said.

'They've gone now.'

'Well, it's time we went too.'

We set off down the winding path, with Rakesh leading the way, and then we had to wait because Dolly had stopped and was waving to someone.

'Who are you waving to, Dolly?'

'To the children.'

'Where are they?'

'Under the chestnut tree.'

'I can't see them. Can you see them, Rakesh? Can you, Mukesh?'

Rakesh and Mukesh said they couldn't see any children. But Dolly was still waving.

'Goodbye,' she called. 'Goodbye!'

Were there voices on the wind? Faint voices calling

goodbye? Could Dolly see something we couldn't see?

'We can't see anyone,' I said.

'No,' said Dolly. 'But they can see me!'

Then she left off her game and joined us, and we ran home laughing. Mrs Williams may not have revisited her old house that day but perhaps her children had been there, playing under the chestnut tree they had known so long ago.

Dragon in the Tunnel

The first time I saw a train, I was standing on a wooded slope outside a tunnel, not far from Kalka. Suddenly, with a shrill whistle and great burst of steam, a green and black engine came snorting out of the blackness.

I turned and ran to my father. 'A dragon!' I shouted. 'There's a dragon coming out of its cave!'

Since then, steam engines and dragons have always inspired the same sort of feelings in me—wonder and awe and delight. I would like to see a real dragon one day, green and gold and—because I have always preferred the 'reluctant' sort—rather shy and gentle; but until that day comes, I shall be content with steam engines.

In India the steam engine is still very much with us. In 1855 the East India Railway was opened between Calcutta and Raniganj, a distance of 122 miles. By the turn of the century, India had one of the most extensive railway systems in the world. Today, the hundreds of trains that criss-cross the subcontinent, panting over the desert and plain, through hill and forest, are still pulled by these snorting monsters who belch smoke by day and scatter red stars in the night.

Even now, when I see a train coming around the bend of

a hill, on crossing a bridge, or cutting across a wide flat plain, I feel the same sort of innocent wonder that I felt as a boy. Where are all these people going to, and where have they come from, and what are they really like? When children wave to me from carriage windows I wave back to them. It is a habit I have never lost. And sometimes I am in a train, waving, and the children from the nearby villages come running out of their mud huts to wave back to me—well, not to me exactly, it is really the train they are waving to…

Small wayside stations have always fascinated me. Manned sometimes by just one or two railway employees, and often situated in the middle of a damp subtropical forest, or clinging to the mountainside on the way to Simla or Darjeeling, these little stations are, for me, outposts of romance, lonely symbols of the pioneering spirit that led men to lay tracks into the remote corners of the earth.

I remember such a stop on a line that went through the Terai forests near the foothills of the Himalayas. At about ten at night, the khilasi, or station watchman, lit his kerosene lamp and started walking up the tracks into the jungle.

'Where are you going?' I asked.

'To see if the tunnel is clear,' he said. 'The Overland Mail comes in twenty minutes.'

I accompanied him a furlong or two along the track, through a deep cutting which led to the tunnel. Every night, the khilasi walked through the dark tunnel, and then stood outside to wave his lamp to the oncoming train as a signal that the track was clear. If the engine driver did not see the lamp he stopped the train. It always slowed down near the cutting.

Having inspected the tunnel, we stood outside, waiting for the train. It seemed a long time coming. There was no moon, and the dense forest seemed to be trying to crowd us into the narrow cutting. The sounds of the forest came to us—the belling of a sambhur deer and the cry of a jackal told us that perhaps a tiger or a leopard was on the prowl. There were strange, nocturnal bird sounds; and then silence.

The khilasi stood outside the tunnel, trimming his lamp, listening to the faint sounds of the jungle—sounds which only he could identify and understand. Something made him stand very still for a few moments, peering into the darkness, and I knew that everything was not as it should be.

'There is something in the tunnel,' he said.

I could hear nothing at first, but then there came a regular sawing sound, just like the sound made by someone sawing through the branch of a tree.

'Baghera!' whispered the khilasi. He had said enough to enable me to recognize the sound—the sawing of a leopard trying to find its mate. 'The train will be coming soon. We must drive the animal out, or it will be run over!'

He must have sensed my surprise, because he said, 'Do not be afraid…I know this leopard well. We have seen each other many times. He has a weakness for stray dogs and goats, but he will not harm us.' He gave me his small handaxe to hold and, raising his lamp high, started walking into the tunnel, shouting at the top of his voice to try and scare away the animal. I followed close behind him.

We had gone about twenty yards into the tunnel when the light from the lamp fell on the leopard, which was crouching between the tracks, only about twenty feet away from us. It bared its teeth in a snarl and went down on its stomach, tail twisting. I thought it was going to spring. The khilasi and I both shouted together. Our voices rang and echoed through the tunnel. And the leopard, uncertain as to how many humans were in there with him, turned swiftly and disappeared into the darkness ahead.

The khilasi and I walked on till the end of the tunnel without seeing the leopard again. As we returned to the entrance of the tunnel the rails began to hum and we knew the train was coming.

I put my hand to one of the rails and felt its tremor. And then the engine came round the bend, hissing at us, scattering sparks into the darkness, defying the jungle as it roared through the steep sides of the cutting. It charged straight at the tunnel and into it, thundering past us like the beautiful dragon of my dreams.

And when it had gone, the silence returned and the forest breathed again. Only the rails still trembled with the passing of the train.

A Station for Scandal

Simla, even in the days of Mrs Hauksbee, was never so promiscuous. Simla, after all, was teeming with officials and empire-builders and ambitious young civil servants. If there wasn't room for them in Simla, they went to Nainital, capital of the United Provinces.

But Mussoorie was non-official.

It was not a summer capital. You could live there without feeling that the Viceroy or the Governor was looking over your shoulder. Those who made their way to Mussoorie did so in order to get as far as possible from viceroys and governors. It was where you went to 'do your own thing', indulge a secret love, or build a cottage for your mistress, far from the stern and censorious eyes of your superior officers. And sometimes the superior officers turned up too, hoping to get away from their junior officer. And if ever the twain met, well, they looked the other way...

Mussoorie is smaller than Simla, all length and no breadth, but from Clouds End in the west to Jabarkhet in the east, it is all of twelve miles, straddling the ridge overlooking the two great rivers, the Ganga and the Jamuna, which are silver slipstreams across the plains below. There is room enough for private lives, for discreet affairs conducted over picnic baskets set down beneath the deodars.

Some years ago I received a letter from a reader in England, wanting to know if there were any Maxwells still living in Mussoorie. He was a Maxwell himself, he said, by his father's first marriage. From what he knew of the family history, there ought to have been several Maxwells by the second marriage, and he wanted to get in touch with them.

He was very frank and mentioned that his father had given up a brilliant career in the Indian Civil Service to marry a fifteen-year-old Muslim girl. He had met the girl in Madras, changed his religion to facilitate the marriage, and then—to avoid 'scandal'—had made his home with her in Mussoorie. His first wife had returned to England with her children.

Although there are no longer any Maxwells in Mussoorie, my neighbour, Miss Bean confirmed that Mr Maxwell's children from his second wife had in fact grown up on the station, each inheriting a considerable property. The old gentleman is buried in the Mussoorie cemetery. The children emigrated, but one granddaughter returned to Mussoorie a few years ago, on a honeymoon with her fourth husband, thus keeping up the family tradition.

Mussoorie, queen of the hills, took this sort of thing in its stride.

The station's reputation was well established as far back as October 1884, when the correspondent of the Calcutta *Statesman* wrote to his paper:

> Last Sunday a sermon was delivered by the Reverend Mr Hackett, belonging to the Church Mission Society; he chose for his text Ezekiel 18th and 2nd verse; the latter clause, 'The fathers have eaten sour grapes

> and set their children's teeth on edge.' The Reverend gentleman discoursed upon the 'highly immoral tone of society up here, that it far surpassed any other hill station in the scale of morals; that ladies and gentlemen after attending church proceeded to a drinking shop, a restaurant adjoining the Library and there indulged freely in *pegs*, not one but many; that at a fancy Bazaar held this season, a lady stood up on a chair and offered her kisses to gentlemen at Rs 5 each. What would they think of such a state of society at Home? But this was not all. Married ladies and married gents formed friendship and associations which tended to no *good* purpose, and set a bad example.'

The poor Reverend preached to no purpose, and it was perhaps just as well that he was not alive in the year 1933, when a lady stood up at a benefit show and auctioned a single kiss for which a gentleman paid ₹300. (The *Statesman* correspondent had nothing to say on that occasion; his silence was in itself a comment on the changing times.)

Mussoorie was probably at its gayest in the '30s. Ballrooms, skating-rinks and cinema-halls flourished. Beauty salons sprang up along the Mall. An old advertisement in my possession announces the superiority of 'Freda' in the art of permanent waving; she was assisted by Miss Harvey, 'late of "Lucille", Bedford'.

The war was to change all this; and by the time independence came to India, most of the European and Anglo-Indian residents had sold their homes and gone away. Only a few stayed on—elderly folk like Miss Bean, who had spent her life here, and others whose meagre incomes did not permit them to go away.

I wonder what brought me back to Mussoorie. True, I had sometimes been here as a child; and my mother's people had lived in Dehradun, in the valley below. When I returned to India, still a young man in my twenties (I had spent only four years in England), I lived in Delhi and Dehra for a few years; and then, without quite knowing why, I found myself visiting the hill station, calling on the oldest resident, Miss Bean, and being told by her that the upper portion of her cottage was to let. On an impulse, I rented it.

Perhaps I really wanted to come back to my beginnings. Because it was in Mussoorie in 1933 (the Year of the Kissing) that my parents first met and enjoyed a typical hill station affair.

I have a photograph of my father and mother, on horseback, riding along the Camel's Back Road not far from the cemetery gate. He was thirty-six then, and had just given up a tea-estate manager's job; she was barely twenty, taking a nurse's training at the Cottage Hospital, just below Gun Hill. A few months later they were husband and wife, living in the heat and dust of Alwar state. I was not born in Mussoorie, but I am pretty sure I had my beginnings there.

There is something in the air of the place—especially in October and November—that is conducive to romance and passion. Miss Bean told me that as a girl she'd had many suitors, and if she did not marry it was more from procrastination than from being passed over. While on all sides elopements and broken marriages were making hill station life exciting, she managed to remain single. She was probably helped in this by her father's reputation for being a very good shot with pistol and Lee-Enfield rifle. She taught elocution in one of the many schools that flourished (and still flourish) in Mussoorie. There is a protective atmosphere about an English public school; an atmosphere which, although it protects one from the outside world, often exposes one to the hazards within the system.

The schools were not without their own scandals. Mrs Fennimore, the wife of a schoolmaster at Oak Grove, got herself entangled in a defamation suit, each hearing of which grew more and more distasteful to her husband. Unable to stand the whole weary and sordid business, Mr Fennimore hit upon a solution. Loading his revolver, he moved to his wife's bedside and shot her through the head. For no accountable reason he put the weapon under her pillow—obviously no one could have mistaken the death for suicide—and then, going to his study, he leaned over his rifle and shot himself.

Ten years later, in the same school, the headmaster's wife was arrested for attempted murder. She had fired at, and wounded, a junior mistress. The case was later hushed up; the motive remains obscure.

But it was on 25 July 1927, at the height of the season and in the heart of the town, that there took place the double tragedy that set the station agog. It all happened in broad daylight and in a full boarding-house, Zephyr Hall.

Shortly after noon the boarders were startled into brisk activity when a shot rang out from one of the rooms, followed by screams. Other shots followed in quick succession. Those boarders who happened to be in the public rooms or on the verandahs dived for the safety of their own apartments and bolted the doors. One unhappy boarder, however, ignorant of where the man with the gun might be, decided to take no chances and came round a corner with his hands held well above his head—only to run straight into the levelled pistol. Even the man who held it, and who had just shot his own wife, couldn't help laughing.

Mr Owen, the gentleman with the gun, killed his wife, wounded his daughter, and finally shot himself. His was the first Christian cremation in Mussoorie, performed in compliance with his wishes expressed long before his dramatic end.

This event had a strange sequel, at least for me.

Last summer, while I was taking a walk along the Mall, I was stopped by a stranger, a small man with pale-blue eyes and thinning hair. He must have been over sixty. Accompanying him was a woman of about thirty, whom he introduced as his wife. He apologized for detaining me, and said, 'But you look as though you have been here for some time. Can you tell me where Miss Garlah lives?'

Miss Garlah, another old resident, is the Secretary of the Cemetery Committee, 'house-proud', so to speak, because a visiting representative of the British High Commission once declared that the Mussoorie cemetery was the best-kept 'old' cemetery in North India.

I gave directions to the visitor, and then asked him if he was visiting Mussoorie for the first time. He seemed to welcome the enquiry and showed an eagerness to talk.

'It's nearly fifty years since I was last here,' he said. And he gestured towards the ruins of Zephyr Hall, once the most fashionable boarding-house in the hill station and now occupied by poor squatters and their families. 'That was where we lived for a couple of years. That was where my poor mother died...'

My mind was alive with conjecture and now something seemed to fall into place. 'Not—not Mrs Owen?' I ventured to ask.

'That's right. But surely you're too young to remember.'

'I heard about it,' I lied. Actually, I had a couple of old newspaper clippings on the case.

'My father had a sudden brainstorm. He shot and killed

my mother. My sister was badly wounded, but she recovered.'

'And what about you?' I asked. I couldn't remember reading about a son.

'I was at school in England, just fourteen years old. They'd sent me to England only a few months before it happened. I heard about it much later. Naturally, I couldn't attend my mother's funeral, and I've had to wait fifty years before I could come and see her grave. I know she'd have wanted me to come.'

He took my telephone number and promised to look me up before he left Mussoorie. But I did not see him again. After a few days I began to wonder if I had really met the survivor of a fifty-year-old tragedy, or if he had been just another of the hill station's ghosts. But only a couple of weeks back, when I was walking along the cemetery's lowest terrace looking for a grave that Miss Garlah said needed to be identified (she couldn't manage the steep path down to the bottom terrace), I received confirmation that Mr Owen junior had indeed visited Mussoorie and that he had found his mother's grave.

There before me was the grave of Mrs Owen, victim of her husband's brainstorm. And a new plaque had been set into the stone, with the inscription: 'Mother Dear, I am Here'.

A Crow for All Seasons

Early to bed and early to rise makes a crow healthy, wealthy and wise.

They say it's true for humans too. I'm not so sure about that. But for crows it's a must.

I'm always up at the crack of dawn, often the first crow to break the night's silence with a lusty caw. My friends and relatives, who roost in the same tree, grumble a bit and mutter to themselves, but they are soon cawing just as loudly. Long before the sun is up, we set off on the day's work.

We do not pause even for the morning wash. Later in the day, if it's hot and muggy, I might take a dip in some human's bath water; but early in the morning we like to be up and about before everyone else. This is the time when trash cans and refuse dumps are overflowing with goodies, and we like to sift through them before the dustmen arrive in their disposal trucks.

Not that we are afraid of a famine in refuse. As human beings multiply, so does their rubbish.

Only yesterday I rescued an old typewriter ribbon from the dustbin, just before it was emptied. What a waste that would have been! I had no use for it myself, but I gave it to one of my cousins who got married recently, and she tells me it's just right for her nest, the one she's building on a telegraph pole. It helps her bind the twigs together, she says.

My own preference is for toothbrushes. They're just a hobby, really, like stamp-collecting is with humans. I have a small but select collection which I keep in a hole in the garden wall. Don't ask me how many I've got—crows don't believe there's any point in counting beyond two—but I know there's more than one, that there's a whole lot of them in fact, because there isn't anyone living on this road who hasn't lost a toothbrush to me at some time or another.

We crows living in the jackfruit tree have this stretch of road to ourselves, but so that we don't quarrel or have misunderstandings we've shared the houses out. I picked the bungalow with the orchard at the back. After all, I don't eat rubbish and throwaways all the time. Just occasionally I like a ripe guava or the soft flesh of a papaya. And sometimes I like the odd beetle as an *hors d'oeuvre*. Those humans in the bungalow should be grateful to me for keeping down the population of fruit-eating beetles, and even for recycling their refuse; but no, humans are never grateful. No sooner do I settle in one of their guava trees than stones are whizzing past me. So, I return to the dustbin on the back verandah steps. They don't mind my being there.

One of my cousins shares the bungalow with me, but he's a lazy fellow and I have to do most of the foraging. Sometimes I get him to lend me a claw, but most of the time he's preening his feathers and trying to look handsome for a pretty young thing who lives in the banyan tree at the next turning.

When he's in the mood he can be invaluable, as he proved recently when I was having some difficulty getting at the dog's food on the verandah.

This dog who is fussed over so much by the humans I've adopted is a great big fellow, a Mastiff who pretends to a pedigree going back to the time of Genghis Khan—he likes to pretend one of his ancestors was the great Khan's watchdog—but, as often happens in famous families, animal or human, there is a falling off in quality over a period of time, and this huge fellow—Tiger, they call him—is a case in point. All brawn and no brain. Many's the time I've removed a juicy bone from his plate or helped myself to pickings from under his nose.

But of late he's been growing canny and selfish. He doesn't like to share any more. And the other day I was almost in his jaws when he took a sudden lunge at me. Snap went his great teeth; but all he got was one of my tail feathers. He spat it out in disgust. Who wants crow's meat, anyway?

All the same, I thought, I'd better not be too careless. It's not for nothing that a crow's IQ is way above that of all other birds. And it's higher than a dog's, I bet.

I woke Cousin Slow from his midday siesta and said, 'Hey, Slow, we've got a problem. If you want any of that delicious tripe today, you've got to lend a claw—or a beak. That dog's getting snappier day by day.'

Slow opened one eye and said, 'Well, if you insist. But you know how I hate getting into a scuffle. It's bad for the gloss on my feathers.'

'I don't insist,' I said politely, 'but I'm not foraging for both of us today. It's every crow for himself.'

'Okay, okay, I'm coming,' said Slow, and with barely a flap he dropped down from the tree to the wall.

'What's the strategy?' I asked.

'Simple. We'll just give him the old one-two.'

We flew across to the verandah. Tiger had just started his meal. He was a fast, greedy eater who made horrible slurping sounds while he guzzled his food. We had to move fast if we wanted to get something before the meal was over.

I sidled up to Tiger and wished him good afternoon.

He kept on gobbling—but quicker now.

Slow came up from behind and gave him a quick peck near the tail—a sensitive spot—and, as Tiger swung round, snarling, I moved in quickly and snatched up several tidbits.

Tiger went for me, and I flew freestyle for the garden wall. The dish was untended, so Slow helped himself to as many scraps as he could stuff in his mouth.

He joined me on the garden wall, and we sat there feasting, while Tiger barked himself hoarse below.

'Go catch a cat,' said Slow, who is given to slang. 'You're in the wrong league, big boy.'

The great sage Pratyasataka—ever heard of him? I guess not—once said, 'Nothing can improve a crow.'

Like most human sages, he wasn't very clear in his thinking, so that there has been some misunderstanding about what he meant. Humans like to think that what he really meant was that crows were so bad as to be beyond improvement. But we crows know better. We interpret the saying as meaning that the crow is so perfect that no improvement is possible.

It's not that when we aren't human—what I mean is, there are times when we fall from our high standards and do rather foolish things. Like at lunch time the other day.

Sometimes, when the table is laid in the bungalow, and before the family enters the dining room, I nip in through the open window and make a quick foray among the dishes. Sometimes I'm lucky enough to pick up a sausage or a slice of toast, or even a pat of butter, making off before someone enters and throws a bread knife at me. But on this occasion, just as I was reaching for the toast, a thin slouching fellow—Junior

Sahib they call him—entered suddenly and shouted at me. I was so startled that I leapt across the table seeking shelter. Something flew at me, and in an effort to dodge the missile I put my head through a circular object and then found it wouldn't come off.

It wasn't safe to hang around there, so I flew out the window with this dashed ring still round my neck.

Serviette or napkin rings, that's what they are called. Quite unnecessary objects, but some humans—particularly the well-to-do sort—seem to like having them on their tables, holding bits of cloth in place. The cloth is used for wiping the mouth. Have you ever heard of such nonsense?

Anyway, there I was with a fat napkin ring round my neck, and as I perched on the wall trying to get it off, the entire human family gathered on their verandah to watch me.

There was the Colonel Sahib and his wife, the Memsahib; there was the scrawny Junior Sahib (worst of the lot); there was a mischievous boy (the Colonel Sahib's grandson) known as the Baba; and there was the cook (who usually flung orange peels at me) and the gardener (who once tried to decapitate me with a spade), and the dog Tiger who, like most dogs, tries unsuccessfully to be human.

Today they weren't cursing and shaking their fists at me; they were just standing and laughing their heads off. What's so funny about a crow with its head stuck in a napkin ring?

Worse was to follow.

The noise had attracted the other crows in the area, and if there's one thing crows detest, it's a crow who doesn't look like a crow.

They swooped low and dived on me, hammering at the wretched napkin ring, until they had knocked me off the wall and into a flower bed. Then six or seven toughs landed on me with every intention of finishing me off.

'Hey, boys!' I cawed. 'This is me, Speedy! What are you trying to do—kill me?'

'That's right! You don't look like Speedy to us. What have you done with him, hey?'

And they set upon me with even greater vigour.

'You're just like a bunch of lousy humans!' I shouted. 'You're no better than them—this is just the way they carry on amongst themselves!'

That brought them to a halt. They stopped trying to peck me to pieces, and stood back, looking puzzled. The napkin ring had been shattered in the onslaught and had fallen to the ground.

'Why, it's Speedy!' said one of the gang.

'None other!'

'Good old Speedy—what are you doing here? And where's the guy we were hammering just now?'

There was no point in trying to explain things to them. Crows are like that. They're all good pals—until one of them tries to look different. Then he could be just another bird.

'He took off for Tibet,' I said. 'It was getting unhealthy for him around here.'

◆

Summertime is here again. And although I'm a crow for all seasons, I must admit to a preference for the summer months.

Humans grow lazy and don't pursue me with so much vigour. Garbage cans overflow. Food goes bad and is constantly being thrown away. Overripe fruit gets tastier by the minute. If fellows like me weren't around to mop up all these unappreciated riches, how would humans manage?

There's one character in the bungalow, the Junior Sahib, who will never appreciate our services, it seems. He simply hates crows. The small boy may throw stones at us occasionally, but then, he's the sort who throws stones at almost anything. There's nothing personal about it. He just throws stones on principle.

The Memsahib is probably the best of the lot. She often throws me scraps from the kitchen—onionskins, potato peels, crusts, and leftovers—and even when I nip in and make off with something not meant for me (like a jam tart or a cheese pakora) she is quite sporting about it. The Junior Sahib looks outraged, but the lady of the house says, 'Well, we've all got to make a living somehow, and that's how crows make theirs. It's high time you thought of earning a living.' Junior Sahib's her nephew—that's his occupation. He has never been known to work.

The Colonel Sahib has a sense of humour but it's often directed at me. He thinks I'm a comedian.

He discovered I'd been making off with the occasional egg from the egg basket on the verandah, and one day, without my knowledge, he made a substitution.

Right on top of the pile I found a smooth round egg, and before anyone could shout 'Crow!' I'd made off with it. It was abnormally light. I put it down on the lawn and set about cracking it with my strong beak, but it would keep slipping away or bounding off into the bushes. Finally, I got it between my feet and gave it a good hard whack. It burst open, to my utter astonishment there was nothing inside!

I looked up and saw the old man standing on the verandah, doubled up with laughter.

'What are you laughing at?' asked the Memsahib, coming out to see what it was all about.

'It's that ridiculous crow!' guffawed the Colonel, pointing at me. 'You know he's been stealing our eggs. Well, I placed a ping pong ball on top of the pile, and he fell for it! He's been struggling with that ball for twenty minutes! That will teach him a lesson.'

It did. But I had my revenge later, when I pinched a brand new toothbrush from the Colonel's bathroom.

The Junior Sahib has no sense of humour at all. He idles about the house and grounds all day, whistling or singing to himself.

'Even that crow sings better than Uncle,' said the boy.

A truthful boy; but all he got for his honesty was a whack on the head from his uncle.

Anyway, as a gesture of appreciation, I perched on the garden wall and gave the family a rendering of my favourite crow song, which is my own composition. Here it is, translated for your benefit:

Oh, for the life of a crow!
A bird who's in the know.
Although we are cursed,
We are never dispersed—
We're always on the go!
I know I'm a bit of a rogue
(And my voice wouldn't pass for a brogue),
But there's no one as sleek
Or as neat with his beak
So they're putting my picture in Vogue!
Oh, for the life of a crow!
I reap what I never sow,
They call me a thief—
Pray I'll soon come to grief—

But there's no getting rid of a crow!

I gave it everything I had, and the humans—all of them on the lawn to enjoy the evening breeze, listened to me in silence, struck with wonder at my performance.

When I had finished, I bowed and preened myself, waiting for the applause.

They stared at each other for a few seconds. Then the Junior Sahib stooped, picked up a bottle opener, and flung it at me.

Well, I ask you!

What can one say about humans? I do my best to defend them from all kinds of criticism, and this is what I get for my pains.

Anyway, I picked up the bottle opener and added it to my collection of odds and ends.

It was getting dark, and soon everyone was stumbling around, looking for another bottle opener. Junior Sahib's popularity was even lower than mine.

One day, Junior Sahib came home carrying a heavy shotgun. He pointed it at me a few times and I dived for cover. But he didn't fire. Probably I was out of range.

'He's only threatening you,' said Slow from the safety of the jamun tree, where he sat in the shadows. 'He probably doesn't know how to fire the thing.'

But I wasn't taking any chances. I'd seen a sly look on Junior Sahib's face, and I decided that he was trying to make me careless. So, I stayed well out of range.

Then one evening I received a visit from my cousin, Charm. He'd come to me for a loan. He wanted some new bottle tops for his collection and had brought me a mouldy old toothbrush to offer in exchange.

Charm landed on the garden wall, toothbrush in his beak,

and was waiting for me to join him there, when there was a flash and a tremendous bang. Charm was sent several feet into the air, and landed limp and dead in a flowerbed.

'I've got him, I've got him!' shouted Junior Sahib. 'I've shot that blasted crow!'

Throwing away the gun, Junior Sahib ran out into the garden, overcome with joy. He picked up my fallen relative, and began running around the bungalow with his trophy.

The rest of the family had collected on the verandah.

'Drop that thing at once!' called the Memsahib.

'Uncle is doing a war dance,' observed the boy.

'It's unlucky to shoot a crow,' said the Colonel.

I thought it was time to take a hand in the proceedings and let everyone know that the *right* crow—the one and only Speedy—was alive and kicking. So I swooped down the jackfruit tree, dived through Junior Sahib's window, and emerged with one of his socks.

Triumphantly flaunting his dead crow, Junior Sahib came dancing up the garden path, then stopped dead when he saw me perched on the window sill, a sock in my beak. His jaw fell, his eyes bulged; he looked like the owl in the banyan tree.

'You shot the wrong crow!' shouted the Colonel, and everyone roared with laughter.

Before Junior Sahib could recover from the shock, I took off in a leisurely fashion and joined Slow on the wall.

Junior Sahib came rushing out with the gun, but by now it was too dark to see anything, and I heard the Memsahib telling the Colonel, 'You'd better take that gun away before he does himself a mischief.' So the Colonel took Junior indoors and gave him a brandy.

I composed a new song for Junior Sahib's benefit, and sang it to him outside his window early next morning:

I understand you want a crow
To poison, shoot or smother;
My fond salaams, but by your leave
I'll substitute another;
Allow me then, to introduce
My most respected brother.

Although I was quite understanding about the whole tragic mixup—I was, after all, the family's very own house crow—my fellow crows were outraged at what happened to Charm, and swore vengeance on Junior Sahib.

'*Carves splendens!*' they shouted with great spirit, forgetting that this title had been bestowed on us by a human.

In times of war, we forget how much we owe to our enemies.

Junior Sahib had only to step into the garden, and several crows would swoop down on him, screeching and swearing and aiming lusty blows at his head and hands. He took to coming out wearing a sola topi, and even then they knocked it off and drove him indoors. Once he tried lighting a cigarette on the verandah steps, when Slow swooped low across the porch and snatched it from his lips.

Junior Sahib shut himself up in his room, and smoked countless cigarettes—a sure sign that his nerves were going to pieces.

Every now and then the Memsahib would come out and shoo us off; and because she wasn't an enemy, we obliged by retreating to the garden wall. After all, Slow and I depended on her for much of our board if not for our lodging. But Junior Sahib had only to show his face outside the house, and all the crows in the area would be after him like avenging furies.

'It doesn't look as though they are going to forgive you,' said the Memsahib.

'Elephants never forget, and crows never forgive,' said the Colonel.

'Would you like to borrow my catapult, Uncle?' asked the boy. 'Just for self-protection, you know.'

'Shut up,' said Junior Sahib and went to bed.

One day, he sneaked out of the back door and dashed across to the garage. A little later the family's old car, seldom used, came out of the garage with Junior Sahib at the wheel. He'd decided that if he couldn't take a walk in safety he'd go for a drive. All the windows were up.

No sooner had the car turned into the driveway than about a dozen crows dived down on it, crowding the bonnet and flapping in front of the windscreen. Junior Sahib couldn't see a thing. He swung the steering wheel left, right and centre, and the car went off the driveway, ripped through a hedge, crushed a bed of sweetpeas and came to a stop against the trunk of a mango tree.

Junior Sahib just sat there, afraid to open the door. The family had to come out of the house and rescue him.

'Are you all right?' asked the Colonel.

'I've bruised my knees,' said Junior Sahib.

'Never mind your knees,' said the Memsahib, gazing around at the ruin of her garden. 'What about my sweetpeas?'

'I think your uncle is going to have a nervous breakdown,' I heard the Colonel saying.

'What's that?' asked the boy. 'Is it the same as a car having a breakdown?'

'Well—not exactly... But you could call it a mind breaking up.'

Junior Sahib had been refusing to leave his room or take

his meals. The family was worried about him. I was worried, too. Believe it or not, we crows are among the very few who sincerely desire the preservation of the human species.

'He needs a change,' said the Memsahib.

'A rest cure,' said the Colonel sarcastically. 'A rest from doing nothing.'

'Send him to Switzerland,' suggested the boy.

'We can't afford that. But we can take him up to a hill station.'

The nearest hill station was some fifty miles as the human drives (only ten as the crow flies). Many people went up during the summer months. It wasn't fancied much by crows. For one thing, it was a tidy sort of place, and people lived in houses that were set fairly far apart. Opportunities for scavenging were limited. Also it was rather cold and the trees were inconvenient and uncomfortable. A friend of mine who had spent a night in a pine tree said he hadn't been able to sleep because of prickly pine needles and the wind howling through the branches.

'Let's all go up for a holiday,' said the Memsahib. 'We can spend a week in a boarding house. All of us need a change.'

A few days later the house was locked up, and the family piled into the old car and drove off to the hills.

I had the grounds to myself.

The dog had gone too, and the gardener spent all day dozing in his hammock. There was no one around to trouble me.

'We've got the whole place to ourselves,' I told Slow.

'Yes, but what good is that? With everyone gone, there are no throwaways, giveaways and takeaways!'

'We'll have to try the house next door.'

'And be driven off by the other crows? That's not our territory, you know. We can go across to help them, or to ask for their help, but we're not supposed to take their pickings. It isn't just cricket, old boy.'

We could have tried the bazaar or the railway station, where there is always a lot of rubbish to be found, but there is also a lot of competition in those places. The station crows are gangsters. The bazaar crows are bullies. Slow and I had grown soft. We'd have been no match for the bad boys.

'I've just realized how much we depend on humans,' I said.

'We could go back to living in the jungle,' said Slow.

'No, that would be too much like hard work. We'd be living on wild fruit most of the time. Besides, the jungle crows won't have anything to do with us now. Ever since we took up with humans, we became the outcasts of the bird world.'

'That means we're almost human.'

'You might say we have all their vices and none of their virtues.'

'Just a different set of values, old boy.'

'Like eating hens' eggs instead of crows' eggs. That's something in their favour. And while you're hanging around here waiting for the mangoes to fall, I'm off to locate our humans.'

Slow's beak fell open. He looked like—well, a hungry crow.

'Don't tell me you're going to follow them up to the hill station? You don't even know where they are staying.'

'I'll soon find out,' I said, and took off for the hills.

You'd be surprised at how simple it is to be a good detective, if only you put your mind to it. Of course, if Ellery Queen had been able to fly, he wouldn't have required fifteen chapters and his father's assistance to crack a case.

Swooping low over the hill station, it wasn't long before I spotted my humans' old car. It was parked outside a hoarding house called Climber's Rest. I hadn't seen anyone climbing, but dozing in an armchair in the garden was my favourite human.

I perched on top of a colourful umbrella and waited for Junior Sahib to wake up. I decided it would be rather inconsiderate of me to disturb his sleep, so I waited patiently on the brolly, looking at him with one eye and keeping one eye on the house. He stirred uneasily, as though he'd suddenly had a bad dream; then he opened his eyes. I must have been the first thing he saw.

'Good morning,' I cawed, in a friendly tone—always ready to forgive and forget, that's Speedy!

He leapt out of the armchair and ran into the house, hollering at the top of his voice.

I supposed he hadn't been able to contain his delight at seeing me again. Humans can be funny that way. They'll hate you one day and love you the next.

Well, Junior Sahib ran all over the boarding house, screaming: 'It's that crow, it's that crow! He's following me everywhere!'

Various people, including the family, ran outside to see what the commotion was about, and I thought it would be better to make myself scarce. So I flew to the top of a spruce tree and stayed very still and quiet.

'Crow! What crow?' said the Colonel.

'Our crow!' cried, Junior Sahib. 'The one that persecutes me. I was dreaming of it just now, and when I opened my eyes, there it was, on the garden umbrella!'

'There's nothing there now,' said the Memsahib. 'You probably hadn't woken up completely.'

'He is having illusions again,' said the boy.

'Delusions,' corrected the Colonel.

'Now look here,' said the Memsahib, 'you'll have to pull yourself together. You'll take leave of your senses if you don't.'

'I tell you, it's here!' sobbed Junior Sahib. 'It's following me everywhere.'

'It's grown fond of Uncle,' said the boy. 'And it seems Uncle can't live without crows.'

Junior Sahib looked up with a wild glint in his eye.

'That's it!' he cried. 'I can't live without them. That's the answer to my problem. I don't hate crows—I love them!'

Everyone just stood around goggling at Junior Sahib.

'I'm feeling fine now,' he carried on. 'What a difference it makes if you can just do the opposite of what you've been doing before! I thought I hated crows. But all the time I really loved them!' And flapping his arms, and trying to caw like a crow, he went prancing about the garden.

'Now he thinks he's a crow,' said the boy. 'Is he still having delusions?'

'That's right,' said the Memsahib. 'Delusions of grandeur.'

After that, the family decided that there was no point in staying on in the hill station any longer. Junior Sahib had completed his rest cure. And even if he was the only one who believed himself cured, that was all right, because after all he was the one who mattered... If you're feeling fine, can there be anything wrong with you?

No sooner was everyone back in the bungalow than Junior Sahib took to hopping barefoot on the grass early every morning, all the time scattering food about for the crows. Bread, chappattis, cooked rice, curried eggplants, the Memsahib's homemade toffee—you name it, we got it!

Slow and I were the first to help ourselves to these dawn offerings, and soon the other crows had joined us on the lawn. We didn't mind. Junior Sahib brought enough for everyone.

'We ought to honour him in some way,' said Slow.

'Yes, why not?' said I. 'There was someone else, hundreds

of years ago, who fed the birds. They followed him wherever he went.'

'That's right. They made him a saint. But as far as I know, he didn't feed any crows. At least, you don't see any crows in the pictures—just sparrows, robins and wagtails.'

'Small fry. *Our* human is dedicated exclusively to crows. Do you realize that, Slow?'

'Sure. We ought to make him the patron saint of crows. What do you say, fellows?'

'Caw, caw, caw!' All the crows were in agreement.

'St Corvus!' said Slow as Junior Sahib emerged from the house, laden with good things to eat.

'Corvus, corvus, corvus!' we cried.

And what a pretty picture he made—a crow eating from his hand, another perched on his shoulder, and about a dozen of us on the grass, forming a respectful ring around him.

From persecutor to protector; from beastliness to saintliness. And sometimes it can be the other way round: you never know with humans!

The Monkeys

I couldn't be sure, next morning, if I had been dreaming or if I had really heard dogs barking in the night and had seen them scampering about on the hillside below the cottage. There had been a golden Cocker, a Retriever, a Peke, a Dachshund, a black Labrador and one or two nondescripts. They had woken me with their barking shortly after midnight, and had made so much noise that I had got out of bed and looked out of the open window. I saw them quite plainly in the moonlight, five or six dogs rushing excitedly through the bracket and long monsoon grass.

It was only because there had been so many breeds among the dogs that I felt a little confused. I had been in the cottage only a week, and I was already on nodding or speaking terms with most of my neighbours. Colonel Fanshawe, retired from the Indian army, was my immediate neighbour. He did keep a Cocker, but it was black. The elderly Anglo-Indian spinsters who lived beyond the deodars kept only cats. (Though why cats should be the prerogative of spinsters, I have never been able to understand.) The milkman kept a couple of mongrels. And the Punjabi industrialist who had bought a former prince's palace—without ever occupying it—left the property in charge of a watchman who kept a huge Tibetan Mastiff.

None of these dogs looked like the ones I had seen in the night.

'Does anyone here keep a Retriever?' I asked Colonel Fanshawe, when I met him taking his evening walk.

'No one that I know of,' he said and gave me a swift, penetrating look from under his bushy eyebrows. 'Why, have you seen one around?'

'No, I just wondered. There are a lot of dogs in the area, aren't there?'

'Oh, yes. Nearly everyone keeps a dog here. Of course, every now and then a panther carries one off. Lost a lovely little terrier myself only last winter.'

Colonel Fanshawe, tall and red-faced, seemed to be waiting for me to tell him something more—or was he just taking time to recover his breath after a stiff uphill climb?

That night I heard the dogs again. I went to the window and looked out. The moon was at the full, silvering the leaves of the oak trees.

The dogs were looking up into the trees and barking. But I could see nothing in the trees, not even an owl.

I gave a shout, and the dogs disappeared into the forest.

Colonel Fanshawe looked at me expectantly when I met him the following day. He knew something about those dogs, of that I was certain; but he was waiting to hear what I had to say. I decided to oblige him.

'I saw at least six dogs in the middle of the night,' I said. 'A Cocker, a Retriever, a Peke, a Dachshund and two mongrels. Now, Colonel, I'm sure you must know whose they are.'

The colonel was delighted. I could tell by the way his eyes glinted that he was going to enjoy himself at my expense.

'You've been seeing Miss Fairchild's dogs,' he said with smug satisfaction.

'Oh, and where does she live?'

'She doesn't, my boy. Died fifteen years ago.'

'Then what are her dogs doing here?'

'Looking for monkeys,' said the colonel. And he stood back to watch my reaction.

'I'm afraid I don't understand,' I said.

'Let me put it this way,' said the colonel. 'Do you believe in ghosts?'

'I've never seen any,' I said.

'But you have, my boy, you have. Miss Fairchild's dogs died years ago—a Cocker, a Retriever, a Dachshund, a Peke and two mongrels. They were buried on a little knoll under the oaks. Nothing odd about their deaths, mind you. They were all quite old, and didn't survive their mistress very long. Neighbours looked after them until they died.'

'And Miss Fairchild lived in the cottage where I stay? Was she young?'

'She was in her mid-forties, an athletic sort of woman, fond of the outdoors. Didn't care much for men. I thought you knew about her.'

'No, I haven't been here very long, you know. But what was it you said about monkeys? Why were the dogs looking for monkeys?'

'Ah, that's the interesting part of the story. Have you seen the langoor monkeys that sometimes come to eat oak leaves?'

'No.'

'You will, sooner or later. There has always been a band of them roaming these forests. They're quite harmless really, except that they'll ruin a garden if given half a chance... Well, Miss Fairchild fairly loathed those monkeys. She was very keen on her dahlias—grew some prize specimens—but the monkeys would come at night, dig up the plants and eat the dahlia bulbs. Apparently, they found the bulbs much to their liking. Miss Fairchild would be furious. People who are passionately fond of gardening often go off balance when their best plants are ruined—that's only human, I suppose. Miss Fairchild set her dogs on the monkeys whenever she could, even if it was in the middle of the night. But the monkeys simply took to the trees and left the dogs barking.

'Then one day—or rather one night—Miss Fairchild took desperate measures. She borrowed a shotgun and sat up near a window. And when the monkeys arrived, she shot one of them dead.'

The colonel paused and looked out over the oak trees which were shimmering in the warm afternoon sun.

'She shouldn't have done that,' he said.

'Never shoot a monkey. It's not only that they're sacred to Hindus—but they are rather human, you know. Well, I must be getting on. Good day!' And the colonel, having ended his story rather abruptly, set off at a brisk pace through the deodars.

I didn't hear the dogs that night. But the next day I saw the monkeys—the real ones, not ghosts. There were about twenty of them, young and old, sitting in the trees munching oak leaves. They didn't pay much attention to me, and I watched them for some time.

They were handsome creatures, their fur a silver-grey, their tails long and sinuous. They leapt gracefully from tree to tree, and were very polite and dignified in their behaviour towards each other—unlike the bold, rather crude red monkeys of the plains. Some of the younger ones scampered about on the hillside, playing and wrestling with each other like schoolboys.

There were no dogs to molest them—and no dahlias to

tempt them into the garden.

But that night, I heard the dogs again. They were barking more furiously than ever.

'Well, I'm not getting up for them this time,' I mumbled, and pulled the blanket over my ears.

But the barking grew louder, and was joined by other sounds, a squealing and a scuffling.

Then suddenly, the piercing shriek of a woman rang through the forest. It was an unearthly sound, and it made my hair stand up.

I leapt out of bed and dashed to the window.

A woman was lying on the ground, three or four huge monkeys were on top of her, biting her arms and pulling at her throat. The dogs were yelping and trying to drag the monkeys off, but they were being harried from behind by others. The woman gave another bloodcurdling shriek, and I dashed back into the room, grabbed hold of a small axe and ran into the garden.

But everyone—dogs, monkeys and shrieking woman—had disappeared, and I stood alone on the hillside in my pyjamas, clutching an axe and feeling very foolish.

The colonel greeted me effusively the following day.

'Still seeing those dogs?' he asked in a bantering tone.

'I've seen the monkeys too,' I said.

'Oh, yes, they've come around again. But they're real enough, and quite harmless.'

'I know—but I saw them last night with the dogs.'

'Oh, did you really? That's strange, very strange.'

The colonel tried to avoid my eye, but I hadn't quite finished with him.

'Colonel,' I said. 'You never did get around to telling me how Miss Fairchild died.'

'Oh, didn't I? Must have slipped my memory. I'm getting old, don't remember people as well as I used to. But, of course, I remember about Miss Fairchild, poor lady. The monkeys killed her. Didn't you know? They simply tore her to pieces...'

His voice trailed of, and he looked thoughtfully at a caterpillar that was making its way up his walking stick.

'She shouldn't have shot one of them,' he said. 'Never shoot a monkey—they're rather human, you know...'

The Kitemaker

There was but one tree in the street known as Gali Ram Nath—an ancient banyan that had grown through the cracks of an abandoned mosque—and little Ali's kite was caught in its branches. The boy, barefoot and clad only in a torn shirt, ran along the cobbled stones of the narrow street to where his grandfather sat nodding dreamily in the sunshine in their back courtyard.

'Grandfather,' shouted the boy. 'My kite has gone!'

The old man woke from his daydream with a start and, raising his head, displayed a beard that would have been white had it not been dyed red with mehendi leaves.

'Did the twine break?' he asked. 'I know that kite twine is not what it used to be.'

'No, Grandfather, the kite is stuck in the banyan tree.'

The old man chuckled. 'You have yet to learn how to fly a kite properly, my child. And I am too old to teach you, that's the pity of it. But you shall have another.'

He had just finished making a new kite from bamboo, paper and thin silk, and it lay in the sun, firming up. It was a pale pink kite with a small green tail. The old man handed it to Ali, and the boy raised himself on his toes and kissed his grandfather's hollowed-out cheek.

'I will not lose this one,' he said. 'This kite will fly like a bird.' And he turned on his heels and skipped out of the courtyard.

The old man remained dreaming in the sun. His kite shop was gone, the premises long since sold to a junk dealer; but he still made kites, for his own amusement and for the benefit of his grandson, Ali. Not many people bought kites these days. Adults disdained them, and children preferred to spend their money at the cinema. Moreover, there were not many open spaces left for the flying of kites. The city had swallowed up the open grassland that had stretched from the old fort's walls to the river bank.

But the old man remembered a time when grown men flew kites, and great battles were fought, the kites swerving and swooping in the sky, tangling with each other until the string of one was severed. Then the defeated but liberated kite would float away into the blue unknown. There was a good deal of betting, and money frequently changed hands.

Kite flying was then the sport of kings, and the old man remembered how the nawab himself would come down to the riverside with his retinue to participate in this noble pastime. There was time, then, to spend an idle hour with a gay, dancing strip of paper. Now everyone hurried, in a heat of hope, and delicate things like kites and daydreams were trampled underfoot.

He, Mehmood the kitemaker, had in the prime of his life been well-known throughout the city. Some of his more elaborate kites once sold for as much as three or four rupees each.

At the request of the nawab he had once made a very special kind of kite, unlike any that had been seen in the district. It consisted of a series of small, very light paper discs trailing on a thin bamboo frame. To the end of each disc he fixed a sprig of grass, forming a balance on both sides. The surface of the foremost disc was slightly convex, and a fantastic face was painted on it, having two eyes made of small mirrors. The discs, decreasing in size from head to tail, assumed an undulatory form and gave the kite the appearance of a crawling serpent. It required great skill to raise this cumbersome device from the ground, and only Mehmood could manage it.

Everyone had heard of the 'Dragon Kite' that Mehmood had built, and word went round that it possessed supernatural powers. A large crowd assembled in the open to watch its first public launching in the presence of the nawab.

At the first attempt it refused to leave the ground. The discs made a plaintive, protesting sound, and the sun was trapped in the little mirrors, making the kite a living, complaining creature. Then the wind came from the right direction, and the Dragon Kite soared into the sky, wriggling its way higher and higher, the sun still glinting in its devil eyes. And when it went very high, it pulled fiercely at the twine, and Mehmood's young sons had to help him with the reel. Still the kite pulled, determined to be free, to break loose, to live a life of its own. And eventually it did so.

The twine snapped, the kite leaped away towards the sun, sailing on heavenward until it was lost to view. It was never found again, and Mehmood wondered afterwards if he had made too vivid, too living a thing of the great kite. He did not make another like it. Instead he presented to the nawab a musical kite, one that made a sound like a violin when it rose into the air.

Those were more leisurely, more spacious days. But the nawab had died years ago, and his descendants were almost as poor as Mehmood himself. Kitemakers, like poets, once had their patrons; but now no one knew Mehmood, simply because there were too many people in the gali, and they could not be bothered with their neighbours.

When Mehmood was younger and had fallen sick, everyone in the neighbourhood had come to ask after his health; but now, when his days were drawing to a close, no one visited him. Most of his old friends were dead and his sons had grown up: one was working in a local garage and the other, who was in Pakistan at the time of the Partition, had not been able to rejoin his relatives.

The children who had bought kites from him ten years ago were now grown men, struggling for a living; they did not have time for the old man and his memories. They had grown up in a swiftly changing and competitive world, and they looked at the old kitemaker and the banyan tree with the same indifference.

Both were taken for granted—permanent fixtures that were of no concern to the raucous, sweating mass of humanity that surrounded them. No longer did people gather under the banyan tree to discuss their problems and their plans; only in the summer months did a few seek shelter from the fierce sun.

But there was the boy, his grandson. It was good that Mehmood's son worked close by, for it gladdened the old man's heart to watch the small boy at play in the winter sunshine, growing under his eyes like a young and well-nourished sapling putting forth new leaves each day. There is a great affinity between trees and men. We grow at much the same pace, if we are not hurt or starved or cut down. In our youth we are resplendent creatures, and in our declining years we stoop a little, we remember, we stretch our brittle limbs in the sun, and then, with a sigh, we shed our last leaves.

Mehmood was like the banyan, his hands gnarled and twisted like the roots of the ancient tree. Ali was like the young mimosa planted at the end of the courtyard. In two years, both he and the tree would acquire the strength and confidence of their early youth.

The voices in the street grew fainter, and Mehmood wondered if he was going to fall asleep and dream, as he so often did, of a kite so beautiful and powerful that it would resemble the great white bird of the Hindus—Garuda, Lord Vishnu's mount. He would like to make a wonderful new kite for little Ali. He had nothing else to give the boy.

He heard Ali's voice in the distance, but did not realize that the boy was calling him. The voice seemed to come from very far away.

Ali was at the courtyard door, asking if his mother had as yet returned from the bazaar. When Mehmood did not answer, the boy came forward repeating his question. The sunlight was slanting across the old man's head, and a small white butterfly rested on his flowing beard. Mehmood was silent; and when Ali put his small brown hand on the old man's shoulder, he met with no response. The boy heard a faint sound, like the rubbing of marbles in his pocket.

Suddenly afraid, Ali turned and moved to the door, and then ran down the street shouting for his mother. The butterfly left the old man's beard and flew to the mimosa tree, and a sudden gust of wind caught the torn kite and lifted it in the air, carrying it far above the struggling city into the blind blue sky.